Tropical marginalia

A footnote history of the General History of Brazil by Francisco Adolfo de Varnhagen (1854-1953)

Vitor Claret Batalhone Júnior

1st Edition

GlobalSouth
P R E S S

For more information, please contact info@globalsouthpress.com or go to http://www.globalsouthpress.com/

Tropical marginalia

By BATALHONE, Vitor—1st ed. — 2016

Includes bibliographical references and index.

ISBN: 978-1-943350-47-6

1. History — Brazil

2. History— Reference

3. International Studies — Latin America

To Temístocles Cezar.

The so-called literary canon, a significantly theological term,
was as characteristic of the age of its birth as the railway...
Marilyn Butler.

All the children say!
We don't need another hero
We don't need to know the way home
All we want is life beyond ...
The Thunderdome.
Tina Turner.

Summary

Acknowledgments

First of all, I would like to thank the Federal University of Rio Grande do Sul (UFRGS), the Institute of Philosophy and Human Sciences, the Department of History and its Graduate Program, where this book was originally conceived, as a dissertation for the obtainment of the Master of History's title. I could not forget to thank the Social Sciences and Humanities Sectorial Library, the UFRGS' Central Library, the Brazilian National Library and the Royal Portuguese Reading Cabinet, extending my gratitude to all their staff for the attentive service always provided throughout my research. To the Coordination for the Improvement of Higher Education Personnel (CAPES) for the full funding of this study through the grant of a scholarship. My gratitude to Christian Navas, Nidi Bueno and GlobalSouth Press for all the attention they have given me during this book's editing process.

I owe a lot to the critical readings offered by professors Fabio Kühn, Anderson Vargas, Benito Schmidt, Mara Rodrigues, and Lúcia Paschoal Guimarães. Also I would like to thank Professor Anthony Grafton, whose book *"The Footnote: A Curious History"* was my original and fundamental inspiration to follow the marginal paths of Brazilian historiography's footnotes. To Professor Maria da Gloria, whose studies on Capistrano de Abreu helped me very much at the beginning of my research, and whom I am proud to work with in the Rural Federal University of Rio de Janeiro (UFRRJ) as a fellow Postdoctoral teacher by CAPES PNPD. I cannot find words to express my gratitude for Professor Temístocles Cezar's orientation and friendship, so I dedicate this book to him.

I also would like to thank my colleagues Eliete Tiburski, Juliano Antoniolli, Marina Araújo, Luciana Boeira, Rodrigo Bonaldo, and Evandro dos Santos from the UFRGS History Department whom have also been huge friends. I will be always thankful to Silas Alves and Felipe Prestes for the Mario Kart races I have very often won, for the years living under the same roof, for have become my brothers, for the strong friendship we have heartily forged. To my parents Matilde "Mother" and Vitor "Father", to Venâncio "Brother" (my patron, alter ego, and great friend), and all my family, I faithfully record these words as a sign of gratitude hence they made it all possible with endless support and indescribable love.

Introduction: A house built on sand?

"- Hand down the cakes! Hand the cakes! - You have to give in,
and recognize a master in him" [1]

"Noble and touching life devoted to work and duty!
Great example to follow and worship!" [2]

Writing the history of Brazil in the beginning of the nineteenth century meant adopting the history of the State, the Nation and the Crown as *a guiding perspective for the research*. That is because "once the National State was implanted, the outlining of a profile for the 'Brazilian nation' was mandatory, one that would be able to provide the nation with its own identity in the broadest set of 'Nations', in accordance with the new principles that ruled the social life of the nineteenth century." [3] Thus was founded, in 1838, within the "belly of the national state's consolidation process," the Brazilian Historical and Geographical Institute (IHGB), which was conceived to guide the "reflections on Brazil, performing the task of systematizing a historiographical production able to help design the outlines that would define the Brazilian nation." [4]

According to the keynote speech delivered by the first secretary Januário da Cunha Barbosa on November 25, 1838, "the recently approved statutes of the newly established institution" stated as one

---

1 Capistrano de Abreu about Francisco Adolfo de Varnhagen *História geral do Brasil*. ABREU, J. Capistrano de. *Ensaios e estudos: (crítica e história)*. 1. série. Rio de Janeiro: Sociedade Capistrano de Abreu, 1931, p.215.

2 ABREU, J. Capistrano de. *Ensaios e estudos: (crítica e história)*. 1. série. Rio de Janeiro: Sociedade Capistrano de Abreu, 1931, p.133.

3 GUIMARÃES, Manoel Luiz Salgado. Nação e civilização nos trópicos: o Instituto Histórico e Geográfico Brasileiro e o projeto de uma História Nacional. *Estudos Históricos*. Rio de Janeiro, n. 1, p.5-27, 1988, p.6. We must understand by *guiding perspective*, "*the general outlook in which the past appears as history*" *and makes sense in relation to the experience and practice of human life, directing them. Rüsen, Jörn. Razão histórica. Teoria da história: os fundamentos da ciência histórica*. Brasília: Editora UnB, 2001, p.31-32.

4 GUIMARÃES, Manoel Luiz Salgado. Nação e civilização nos trópicos: o Instituto Histórico e Geográfico Brasileiro e o projeto de uma História Nacional. *Estudos Históricos*. Rio de Janeiro, n. 1, p.5-27, 1988, p.6-7.

of the "core guidelines for the research's development [...] The collection and publication of documents relevant to the history of Brazil"[5]. First it was necessary to discover, collect and gather the necessary documentation. From the 1850s', "the institute began prioritizing the production of new works in the fields of history, geography and ethnology, thus pushing to the background the task of collecting and storing documents, which had hitherto been a priority."[6] Still, writing a general history of Brazil was not a priority in the Brazilian Historical and Geographical Institute program. First of all, the collection of documents and production of various monographic researches on the history of Brazil was considered necessary.

Thus, considering the IHGB as the socially privileged *center* for the Brazilian historical production from the mid-nineteenth century to the first three decades of the twentieth century,[7] this study will be devoted to the work that would later be recognized as the "monument"[8] of Brazilian historiography, namely: *Brazil's General History* written by Francisco Adolfo de Varnhagen, Viscount of Porto Seguro, originally published in two volumes between 1854 and 1857.

---

5 GUIMARÃES, Manoel Luiz Salgado. Nação e civilização nos trópicos: o Instituto Histórico e Geográfico Brasileiro e o projeto de uma História Nacional. *Estudos Históricos*. Rio de Janeiro, n. 1, p.5-27, 1988 p.9.

6 GUIMARÃES, Manoel Luiz Salgado. Nação e civilização nos trópicos: o Instituto Histórico e Geográfico Brasileiro e o projeto de uma História Nacional. *Estudos Históricos*. Rio de Janeiro, n. 1, p.5-27, 1988, p.11.

7 CERTEAU, Michel de. *A escrita da história*. Rio de Janeiro: Forense Universitária, 2006, p.66-77.

8 "The monument has been erected, and as this was the only part of his last wishes that was not met, the eminent Brazilian can now rest satisfied in the tomb that closes on foreign territory. It is a legitimate satisfaction and he won with dignity. In his childhood he had raised thought to a history of their country, and held it. "ABREU, J. Capistrano de. *Ensaios e estudos: (crítica e história)*. 1. série. Rio de Janeiro: Sociedade Capistrano de Abreu, 1931, p.195. Ver também: WEHLING, Arno. *Estado, história, memória: Varnhagen e a construção da identidade nacional*. Rio de Janeiro: Nova Fronteira, 1999, p.186, 193, 195, 203-212; MATTOS, Selma Rinaldi de. *O Brasil em lições: a história como disciplina escolar em Joaquim Manuel de Macedo*. Rio de Janeiro: Access, 2000, p.45, 69-70, 77, 82-85, 107-113; RODRIGUES, José Honório. *História da história do Brasil. A historiografia conservadora*. São Paulo/Brasília: Companhia Editora Nacional / Instituto Nacional do Livro, 1978-1988, p.18, 29-31.

The production of the *Brazilian general history* took place under the auspices of the Historical Institute, thus not deviating from the guiding perspective of national point of view. [9] As Cezar correctly reminded us within the work of Varnhagen "the idea of nation serves as an organizing concept and as a narrative resource."[10] Besides that, the Viscount relied upon great incentives for the discovery of relevant documents to the construction of "Fatherland's History", due to the fact that he was not only a corresponding member for the IHGB in Europe, as Varnhagen was also a career diplomat.[11] During this period, the IHGB received substantial financial resources from the Imperial State, which reached 75% of IHGB's budget. This money was directed especially for the financing "of their special projects, such as exploratory trips, research and collection of materials in foreign archives."[12]

Varnhagen wrote in his "Dedication to the Imperial Majesty, the Lord D. Pedro II" within the second edition of his most popular work, that he has always sought "for the copy of the most ascertained facts, as for the more precise assessment of others, clarified by the discovery of new documents or more accurate tests."[13] So Varnhagen made his *general History of Brazil* on the principle that the largest number of documents collected and made public would make his story more "real," narrating "the facts as they transpired."[14]

---

9   The original is in French. All translations of works here quoted and referenced are the sole responsibility of the author. CEZAR, Themistocles. *L'écriture de l'histoire au Brésil au XIXe siècle: essai sur une rhétorique de la nacionalité: Le cas Varnhagen.* Doctoral thesis. Advisor: Prof. Dr. François Hartog. Paris: EHESS, 2002, p.12-14.

10 CEZAR, Themistocles.*L'écriture de l'histoire au Brésil au XIXe siècle: essai sur une rhétorique de la nacionalité: Le cas Varnhagen.*Doctoral thesis. Advisor: Prof. Dr. François Hartog. Paris: EHESS, 2002, p.576.

11 "Returning to Portugal, appointed attached to our legation, not cool for a moment.(...) In Peru, Venezuela, Cuba, as in St. Petersburg, Stockholm and Rio de Janeiro, everywhere he inhabits, or through, carried by diplomatic duties [. . .]. " ABREU, J. Capistrano de. *Ensaios e estudos: (crítica e história).* 1. série. Rio de Janeiro: Sociedade Capistrano de Abreu, 1931, p.129-131.

12 GUIMARÃES, Manoel Luiz Salgado. Nação e civilização nos trópicos: o Instituto Histórico e Geográfico Brasileiro e o projeto de uma História Nacional. *Estudos Históricos.* Rio de Janeiro, n. 1, p.5-27, 1988, p.9.

13 VARNHAGEN, Francisco Adolfo de. *História geral do Brasil: antes da sua separação e independência de Portugal.* 4.ed. integral. São Paulo: Melhoramentos, 1948-1953, p.V.

14 VARNHAGEN, Francisco Adolfo de. *História geral do Brasil: antes da sua se-*

However, Varnhagen did not get his desired recognition right away. Possibly "Varnhagen's choices in the development of his work, generated, at the time its first volume came out, not the recognition the author expected, but certain silence, especially among IHGB members linked to Indianist writers, who had the sympathy of Emperor".[15] This initial resistance to the acceptance of *general history* by his peers must have stimulated Varnhagen to write within the "Dedications", that "future readers will acknowledge the rich legacy the book has produced. Although still with flaws, it should be seen as the offspring of the hard work of a lifetime, devoted to studying and researching the truth."[16] What was at stake was not just the intellectual honor of Viscount de Porto Seguro, but also the formation of a discipline and a national historical tradition.

In 1854, the Viscount published the first volume of his major work and, in 1857, the second. According to this data, we could assume that the trajectory of *Brazil's general history* had ended in 1857 with the publication of his second volume. But it is important to note that it was over only regarding some aspects. The trajectory of his work had only just begun in 1857. In 1877, a second edition annotated by the author came off the press also in two volumes. In 1907, the first volume of the third annotated edition was published by Capistrano de Abreu. The third and fourth issues annotated by Rodolfo Garcia were published twenty-one years later, not without recognizing in Capistrano the *jus auctoris*.[17] Within this process, the first two volu-

paração e independência de Portugal. 4.ed. integral. São Paulo: Melhoramentos, 1948-1953, p.V., p.238.

15 MOLLO, Helena Miranda. *História Geral do Brasil: entre o espaço e o tempo* In: COSTA, Wilma Peres & OLIVEIRA, Cecília Helena de Salles (Orgs.). *De um Império a outro: formação do Brasil, séculos XVIII e XIX*. São Paulo: Hucitec: Fapesp, 2007, p.101; GUIMARÃES, Lúcia M. Paschoal. Debaixo da Imediata Proteção de Sua Majestade Imperial. O Instituto Histórico e Geográfico Brasileiro (1838-1889). *Revista do Instituto Histórico e Geográfico Brasileiro*. Rio de Janeiro, a.156, v.1, n.388, p.459-613, jul./set., 1995, p.558-561. Text available at http://www.ihgb.org.br/rihgb/rihgb1995numero0388.pdf . Accessed 27/09/2010.

16 VARNHAGEN, Francisco Adolfo. General *history of Brazil: before their separation and independence of Portugal*.4.ed. full. Sao Paulo: Improvements, 1948-1953, p.SAW.

17 "The first edition of the *General History of Brazil*, we have already indicated, was published in two volumes in Madrid between 1854 and 1857, and was particularly read and discussed throughout the nineteenth century, which is why it is the

mes were doubled in size, with a total of four volumes, in other words, the two additional volumes to the first two editions of the book, are basically composed of footnotes and end sections. Thus, despite the initial opposition to the *General History of Brazil* by IHGB's Indianist group, I believe that when Varnhagen published the first edition of his book in Madrid, between 1854 and 1857, he also laid the foundational groundworks of the great monument of national history.[18]

In the late nineteenth century, Capistrano de Abreu exposed, through two important articles, his assessment on some of the most

central object of this analysis,. The second edition, corrected and enlarged, was published in Vienna in 1877, a year before the author's death. Capistrano de Abreu began the publication of a third edition of the work, corrected and annotated by himself in 1906, but he did not finish because of a fire in the publishing house. Rodolfo Garcia took over the project in 1928 and published in five volumes, the third complete edition, with his comments and Capistrano's work on the original text of Varnhagen. " CEZAR, Themistocles. *L'écriture de l'histoire au Brésil au XIXe siècle: essai sur une rhétorique de la nacionalité: Le cas Varnhagen.*Doctoral thesis. Advisor: Prof. Dr. François Hartog. Paris: EHESS, 2002, p.540-541; OLIVEIRA, Maria da Glória. The annotation and writing: about the story into chapters of John Capistrano de Abreu. *History of Historiography,* n.2, p.86-99, sea., 2009. Text available at: http://www.ichs.ufop.br/rhh/index.php/revista/article/viewFile/9/9. Accessed 01/10/2010; GARCIA, Rodolfo. *Explicação.* In: VARNHAGEN, Francisco Adolfo de. *História geral do Brasil: antes da sua separação e independência de Portugal.* 4.ed. integral. São Paulo: Melhoramentos, 1948-1953, p.III.

18 According to the French historian Jacques Le Goff, a monument is a sign, a legacy of the past that "has the features to connect, to power perpetuation, voluntary or involuntary, of historical societies (it is a legacy of collective memory) and resubmit the evidence that only a small portion are written testimonies. "According to the author, after the methodological revolution due to the emergence of modern documentary critical process originated from the impact of the seventeenth century diplomatic treaties such as *De re diplomatic* Dom Jean Mabillon, but without ignoring the *De fake credit et ementita Constantini donatione declamatio* Lorenzo Valla dated 1440, in which Valla proved to be false diplomas on the papal state grant that would have been made by the emperor Constantine, came the possibility of monuments to be transformed into documents. In this way, and through a brief analysis of the transformation that quantitative methods and the use of led to computers to historical studies, Le Goff argued that it was possible to question the power relations inscribed on the composition and selection of monuments / documents, making room for perception of the complex relationships that involve the basic work of the historian, that is, work with sources. LE GOFF, Jacques. *Documento/monumento.* In: *História e memória.* Campinas: Ed.UNICAMP, 2003, p.525-541.

notable authors and works of the incipient Brazilian historiography, among which he focused especially on Varnhagen and João Francisco Lisboa.[19] This review aimed on assessing the guiding perspectives, the conceptions of method for national history's construction, the sources that were used, as well as the theoretical and methodological differences between them. Throughout these texts, Capistrano described what, in his view, was considered the best way to write National History. This activity depended, on its most basic level, on the "screening and rigorous investigation of the sources, indicating the gaps, discussing the facts narrated by their predecessors and, finally, it depended on the comprehensive bibliographic annotation of contemporary documents and recent monographs on the topics being researched."[20]

Within the specific stage of writing this history, Capistrano wanted the narrative to be guided by the "creative set of doctrines that in the recent years have evolved into a science under the name of sociology", the lack of which, according to the historian, was a big gap of the

---

19 Such articles are *Necrológio de Francisco Adolpho de Varnhagen, Visconde de Porto Seguro* e *Sobre o Visconde de Porto Seguro*. O *Necrológio de Francisco Adolpho de Varnhagen, Visconde de Porto Seguro* was originally published on *Jornal do Commercio*, de 16 e 20 de Dezembro de 1878, and reproduced on *Appenso à História Geral do Brasil*, de Varnhagen, tomo 1.º, pg. 502/5ed08, 4.ª ed.. The *Sobre o Visconde de Porto Seguro* was originally published on *Gazeta de Notícias*, do Rio, de 21, 22 e 23 de Novembro de 1882, e reproduzido em *Appenso à História Geral de Varnhagen*, tomo 3.º, pg. 435/444, 3.ª ed.. ABREU, J. Capistrano de. *Ensaios e estudos: (crítica e história)*. 1. série. Rio de Janeiro: Sociedade *According to Oliveira, these articles have already proven the concept of Capistrano on the guiding principles of the writing of national history.* OLIVEIRA, Maria da Glória. *Crítica, método e escrita da história em João Capistrano de Abreu (1853-1927)*. Dissertação de Mestrado. Orientador: Prof. Dr. Temístocles Cezar. Porto Alegre: UFRGS, IFCH - Departamento de História, Programa de Pós-Graduação em História, 2006, p.42, 67; ABREU, J. Capistrano de. *Ensaios e estudos: (crítica e história)*. 1. série. Rio de Janeiro: Sociedade Capistrano de Abreu, 1931, p.138-139, 214-215; *Regarding Capistrano articles 1878 and 1882 and its evaluation character of national historiography of that period, Jose Honorio Rodrigues wrote that "The historiographical criticism was made by Capistrano de Abreu, in two magnificent volumes" [. . .]. "RODRIGUES, Jose Honorio. História e Historiografia Petropolis: Vozes, 1970, p.125.*

20 OLIVEIRA, Maria da Glória. *Crítica, método e escrita da história em João Capistrano de Abreu (1853-1927)*. Dissertação de Mestrado. Orienter: Prof. Dr. Temístocles Cezar. Porto Alegre: UFRGS, IFCH - Departamento de História, Programa de Pós-Graduação em História, 2006, p.104-105.

Viscount's Work.[21] According to Maria da Gloria Oliveira, Capistrano started his historiographical project from these concepts:

> After examining the criticism of what had preceded the National History's study, all that Capistrano could do was to follow their steps in developing his historian tasks. Among these were the procedures identified by me as the *"moment of the filing"* which corresponds to the moment the historiographical operation starts to be written: a process that comprises everything from the documentary work of review and editing of the sources to the constitution of the documentary evidence. Even though Capistrano has formulated his project of a history of Brazil based on "broad strokes and wide stitches," the author would constantly postpone its implementation due to the need of a preliminary survey and extensive study of its fundamental documents.
>
> The primacy attributed by him to the practice of reader/researcher and editor/compiler was justified by the demands of a History that was intended to be more complete than its predecessors. [22]

Despite all his theoretical and methodological refinement and all the critical work dedicated to the sources, Capistrano had not yet decided to write a new history of Brazil. Among his contemporaries, the question prevailed: "Why has Capistrano de Abreu not written a new History of Brazil?" Capistrano was considered "the biggest connoisseur among all researchers devoted to investigate National History, and being Varnhagen's heir, he was expected to fulfill the great historian attributions, presenting a History of Brazil in monumental scale." [23] The reality was different.

Capistrano truly recognized the merits of Varnhagen, he defended that after the publication of his *General History of Brazil,* there was no one else who had presented "the Cyclopean mass of materials

---

21 ABREU, J. Capistrano de. *Ensaios e estudos: (crítica e história).* 1. série. Rio de Janeiro: Sociedade Capistrano de Abreu, 1931, p.139.

22 OLIVEIRA, Maria da Glória. *Crítica, método e escrita da história em João Capistrano de Abreu (1853-1927).* Dissertação de Mestrado. Advisor: Prof. Dr. Temístocles Cezar. Porto Alegre: UFRGS, IFCH - Departamento de História, Programa de Pós-Graduação em História, 2006, p.162.

23 OLIVEIRA, Maria da Glória. *Crítica, método e escrita da história em João Capistrano de Abreu (1853-1927).* Dissertação de Mestrado. Advisor: Prof. Dr. Temístocles Cezar. Porto Alegre: UFRGS, IFCH - Departamento de História, Programa de Pós-Graduação em História, 2006.p.130.

[sources-documents] he accumulated". Furthermore, he advocated that [24] Varnhagen was the first who "always sought and repeatedly managed to assess the actual national point of view."[25] "The establishment of Brazilian historiography *founding pact* would be directly related to the identification of this distinction, described by Capistrano as a "progress" in the way of conceiving National History"[26] Therefore, after his first efforts to publish critical and annotated editions to important sources for the construction of Brazilian history, in order to give his historiographical project a more concrete shape, Capistrano opted for annotating and reviewing Varnhagen's *General History*, once that moment was seen as not yet conducive to the writing of a new general history of Brazil.[27]

Now, the image of the history of Brazil as 'a house built on sand', used by Capistrano at the end of his life, supports the perception of precarious grounds for the construction of a complete history of architecture, which, according to him, has been obliterated by the lack of sources. Thus the urgency in investigating, critically gathering evidence, methodically studying documents before writing History. Thus, the elaboration of the notes to Varnhagen's work serves this purpose, and more than a historian's scholarly exercise, it was presented as a necessary precondition for the writing of his projected history of Brazil.

It was, therefore, not so much about challenging Varnhagen's work, but scrutinizing it, following the trail of its many sources, identifying its origins, confronting them with other testimonials,

24 ABREU, J. Capistrano de. *Ensaios e estudos: (crítica e história)*. 1. série. Rio de Janeiro: Sociedade Capistrano de Abreu, 1931, p.135.

25 ABREU, J. Capistrano de. *Ensaios e estudos: (crítica e história)*. 1. série. Rio de Janeiro: Sociedade Capistrano de Abreu, 1931, p.139.

26 OLIVEIRA, Maria da Glória. *Crítica, método e escrita da história em João Capistrano de Abreu (1853-1927)*. Dissertação de Mestrado. Orientador: Prof. Dr. Temístocles Cezar. Porto Alegre: UFRGS, IFCH - Departamento de História, Programa de Pós-Graduação em História, 2006, p.72.

27 "[. . .] In his critique of Varnhagen, Capistrano formulated the guidelines of a historiographical project. Therefore, it was essential to continue 'building' what started with the work of the Viscount de Porto Seguro, through documentary research and monographic studies. "OLIVEIRA, Maria da Glória. *Crítica, método e escrita da história em João Capistrano de Abreu (1853-1927)*. Dissertação de Mestrado. Orientador: Prof. Dr. Temístocles Cezar. Porto Alegre: UFRGS, IFCH - Departamento de História, Programa de Pós-Graduação em História, 2006, p.87.

in order to rectify it, making his narrative accurate and less incomplete. [28]

According to Capistrano de Abreu, the history of Brazil gave "the impression of a house built on sand. It is like when someone leans against a wall and there comes down the *grampiola*, even though its structure seems reliable," [29] Based in Capistrano's analogy of a "house built on sand", Oliveira wrote:

> The story, to which customarily was incorporated the adjective "national", was designed within Capistrano's early critical essays and corresponded to an arduous project that wouldn't be consummated, not even after the dedication of nearly a lifetime. And in the end, Capistrano sees it as "a house built on sand." Would it be due to the realization that his own project was built on inevitably uncertain basis, or, and also, to the recognition of the paradoxical relationship between the investigated past and the knowledge obtained from it after methodically deciphering its documents? [30]

Unlike what has been proposed, I believe that these "walls", seen as the historiographical productions subsequent to Varnhagen's, may have been fragile, but the problem was not necessarily within their bases, since they have been solidly founded by Viscount and ratified by Capistrano de Abreu and Rodolfo Garcia. In short, this study aims to describe the discursive phenomenon through which a certain structure of the history of Brazil was recognized and consolidated within the

28 OLIVEIRA, Maria da Glória. *Crítica, método e escrita da história em João Capistrano de Abreu (1853-1927)*. Dissertação de Mestrado. Orientador: Prof. Dr. Temístocles Cezar. Porto Alegre: UFRGS, IFCH - Departamento de História, Programa de Pós-Graduação em História, 2006, p.131-132, 153.
29 OLIVEIRA, Maria da Glória. *Crítica, método e escrita da história em João Capistrano de Abreu (1853-1927)*. Dissertação de Mestrado. Orientador: Prof. Dr. Temístocles Cezar. Porto Alegre: UFRGS, IFCH - Departamento de História, Programa de Pós-Graduação em História, 2006, p.51.
30 The emphasis in italics are my responsibility. OLIVEIRA, Maria da Glória. *Crítica, método e escrita da história em João Capistrano de Abreu (1853-1927)*. Dissertação de Mestrado. Orientador: Prof. Dr. Temístocles Cezar. Porto Alegre: UFRGS, IFCH - Departamento de História, Programa de Pós-Graduação em História, 2006, p.51-52.

field of discursive events. That supposed structure persisted, although with rectifications and restructurings, from 1854 - with the first publication of the *General History of Brazil* - until the mid-twentieth century, when such work finally received its last versions annotated and criticized by Rodolfo Garcia. The moments of *discursive dispersion* will be analyzed, in which the choices of what and how the history of Brazil should be written were made by Capistrano and Garcia during this process of adding notes to the *General History of Brazil*. Therefore understanding how the *discursive strategies* of annotators directed their choices of what should be privileged within the process of writing the history of Brazil, establishing Varnhagen as an authority in the production of "National History". The goal here is not to judge if such strategies were conscious, veiled, or even psychologically originated within its agents, but to observe and describe how/why the emergence of a certain group of statements about national history was possible, which we believe to be linked to the recognition of Viscount of Porto Seguro as an authority of national history. We seek to describe which discursive and belief phenomena enabled the emergence of a group of statements about Brazilian history that could be shared by different people at different times in the course of a temporal and phenomenal series, which, although not necessarily continuous, aspired to the idea of continuity. This would enable a better understanding of the Brazilian historiography's shaping process, which started at the nineteenth century, with its methods, theoretical and epistemological concepts, as well as its possibilities of choices and necessary consequences about how to write national history.

Supporting the study proposed here, is the concept of *authority* as stipulated by Hannah Arendt in a study entitled *What is authority?* [31] In this text, Arendt proposes a reflection on the vicissitudes of maintenance and duration of modern political bodies following those suggestions offered by Modern Political Philosophy to justify and legitimize such political bodies that emerged from the decline of Roman Empire and Catholic Church after its crisis at the end of the Middle Ages and beginning of Early Modern times, most notably during at

---

31 ARENDT, Hannah. *Que é Autoridade?* In: *Entre o passado e o futuro*. São Paulo: Perspectiva, 2007, p.127-187.

the seventeenth century.[32] Arendt also elaborates on the intrinsic relationship between the crisis of the Western Greco-Roman's political and institutional tradition, the temporal acceleration phenomenon experienced by historical agents and the consequent change of the concept of *history* in Modern times.[33]

According to Arendt, an *authority* is strictly linked to an original act of foundation. Thus, the author reminds us about the etymological origins of the word "authority" and the historical beginnings of its concept. After the founding of Rome, the Romans first established the word "authority".[34]

---

32 "Unless it is recognized that the Roman *pathos* foundation inspired them, it seems to me that neither the grandeur nor the tragedy of the modern era Western revolutions can be properly understood.(...) For if I am right in suspecting that the crisis in the world today is basically political in nature, and that the famous 'decline of the West' mainly consists of the decline of the Roman trinity of religion, tradition and authority, with the concomitant undermining of the specifically Roman foundations political domain, then the revolutions of modern times seem gigantic attempts to repair these foundations, to renew the thread broken tradition and restore, through founding new political bodies, what for so many centuries has committed to human affairs a measure of dignity and grandeur. " ARENDT, Hannah. *Que é Autoridade?* In: *Entre o passado e o futuro.* São Paulo: Perspectiva, 2007, p.127-187.p.165; I use these great divisions of Western history only to demarcate the phenomenon treated by Arendt, not ignoring its drawbacks, such as the implicit teleological conception in the division between Antiquity - Middle Ages - Modernity. On the formation of the concept *Modernity* and its motion concepts that indicate a change in the perception of the experience of time and the concept of *history*, KOSELLECK, Reinhart. *"Modernidade" – Sobre a semântica dos conceitos de movimento na modernidade* In: *Futuro Passado, Contribuição à semântica dos tempos históricos.* Rio de Janeiro: Contraponto/Ed.PUCRJ, 2006, p.267-303.

33 ARENDT, Hannah. *Que é Autoridade?* In: *Entre o passado e o futuro.* São Paulo: Perspectiva, 2007, p.131-132; on the crisis of the Western cultural tradition and the temporal acceleration phenomenon experienced by historical actors and the consequent amendment of the concept of *history*, see:KOSELLECK, Reinhart. *Futuro Passado, Contribuição à semântica dos tempos históricos.* Rio de Janeiro: Contraponto/Ed.PUCRJ, 2006; _____. *historia/Historia.* Madri: Editorial Trotta, 2004; HARTOG, François. O Tempo desorientado, Tempo e História: "Como escrever a história da França?". *Anos 90: revista do Programa de Pós-Graduação em História.* Porto Alegre, n.7, p.7-28, jul., 1997; _____. *Regimes de historicidade: presentismo e experiências do tempo.* Belo Horizonte: Autêntica, 2013.

34 As Arendt tells us, the *auctoritas* word is derived from the Latin verb *augere*, meaning "increase". ARENDT, Hannah. *Que é Autoridade?* In: *Entre o passado e*

At the heart of Roman politics from the beginning of the Republic until virtually the end of the imperial era, there is the conviction of the sacredness of the foundation, in the sense that, once something has been founded, it remains mandatory for all future generations. Participate in politics meant, first and foremost, to preserve the foundation of Rome.[35]

Arendt then defines the concept of *authority* as a guiding parameter that converts into regulatory standards, certain truths derived from an original act of foundation transformed into self-evident rules that restrained new patterns of action without a prior judgment. [36]

It is in this context that word and concept of authority originally appeared. The word *auctoritas* derives from the verb *augere*, "augment," and what authority or those in authority constantly augment is the foundation. Those endowed with authority were the elders, the Senate or the *patres*, who had obtained it by descent and by transmission (tradition) from those who had laid the foundations for all things to come, the ancestors, whom the Romans therefore called the *maiores*. The authority of the living was always derivative, depending upon the *auctores imperil Romani conditoresque*, as Pliny puts it, upon the authority of the founders, who no longer were among the living. Authority, in contradistinction to power (*potestas*), had its roots in the past, but this past was no less present in the actual life of the city than the power and strength of the living. *Moribus antiquis res stat Romana virisque, in the words of Ennius.*

In order to understand more concretely what it meant to be in authority, it may be useful to notice that the word *auctores* can be used as the very opposite of the *artifices*, the actual builders and makers, and this precisely when the word *auctor* signifies the same thing as our "author." Who, asks Pliny at the occasion of a new theater, should be more admired, the maker or the author, the inventor or the invention? – meaning, of course, the latter in

o futuro. São Paulo: Perspectiva, 2007, p.163.
35 ARENDT, Hannah. *Que é Autoridade?* In: *Entre o passado e o futuro*. São Paulo: Perspectiva, 2007, p.162.
36 ARENDT, Hannah. *Que é Autoridade?* In: *Entre o passado e o futuro*. São Paulo: Perspectiva, 2007, p.147-155.

both instances. The author in this case is not the builder but the one who inspired the whole enterprise and whose spirit, therefore, much more than the spirit of the actual builder, is represented in the building itself. In distinction to the *artifex*, who only made it, he is the actual "author" of the building, namely its founder; with it he has become an "augmenter" of the city.

Mommsen called it "more than advice and less than a command, an advice which one may not safely ignore," whereby it is assumed that "the will and the actions of the people like those of children are exposed to error and mistakes and therefore need 'augmentation' and confirmation through the council of elders." The authoritative character of the "augmentation" of the elders lies in its being a mere advice, needing neither the form of command nor external coercion to make itself heard.[37]

Thus, I use the concept of *authority* defined above by Arendt to elucidate how the process of annotating the *General History of Brazil* conducted by Capistrano de Abreu and Rodolfo Garcia ratified the discursive authority of Varnhagen regarding Brazilian history and historiography. However, by doing this I do not mean this recognition of Varnhagen as the greatest authority on the history of Brazil until the very beginning of twentieth century had been instituted specifically through the annotation of his main work by Garcia and Capistrano. Rather, I would like to suggest that this annotation process worked to reinforce the recognition of Varnhagen's authority within the textual body of his own work, helping to corroborate Varnhagen's discursive conformation of Brazilian national historiography from the mid-nineteenth century until at least the mid-twentieth century.

I therefore consider that Varnhagen founded the "National History" with his "monument", which were "enhanced" due to the footnotes and end of sections credited to "craftsmen" Capistrano and Garcia. The imperative imposed on "artifices" to submit to the "advices" of the founder - these councils being understood as authority that emanates from the choices and achievements of Varnhagen's statements on national history - considering that his "monument" has

---

37 ARENDT, Hannah. *Que é Autoridade?* In: *Entre o passado e o futuro*. São Paulo: Perspectiva, 2007, p.163-165.

embedded his " spirit "- that is, the theoretical and methodological features of such set of statements - does not change the fact that the annotators need to rectify said foundation, once it is necessary to understand the constitution of modern historiography as potentially open over successive and gradual accumulations.[38] For Capistrano, as well as for José Honório Rodrigues, the authority of an author is formed only after a critical review on his work.[39] Such criticism is inherent and necessary to the recognition to every relation of authority. Only then, as suggested by Arendt and Mommsen, it is possible to establish Varnhagen as an *authority* of national history. Once his annotators placed themselves as critical perpetuators of the Viscount's work, they also established themselves as authorities in Brazilian history.

An enunciation, as suggested by Michel Foucault, is "a strange event":

> [. . .] Initially because it is linked, on one hand, to a writing gesture or to the word's articulation, but on the other hand, it gives itself a remnant existence within the field of memory, or in the materiality of manuscripts, books and any form of registration; then because it is unique like every event, but is open to repetition, to transformation, to reactivation; finally, because it is linked not only to situations that cause it, and to the consequences caused by it, but at the same time, and in an entirely different way, it is connected to the statements that precede and follow it.[40]

Therefore, to articulate the concept of *authority* derived from the classical Greco-Roman culture, as defined by Arendt I will also use the concept of *"founder of discursivity"*, established by Foucault. According to the author:

---

38 KOSELLECK, Reinhart. *"Modernidade" – Sobre a semântica dos conceitos de movimento na modernidade* In: *Futuro Passado, Contribuição à semântica dos tempos históricos*. Rio de Janeiro: Contraponto/Ed.PUCRJ, 2006, p.282-296.

39 OLIVEIRA, Maria da Glória. *Crítica, método e escrita da história em João Capistrano de Abreu (1853-1927)*. Dissertação de Mestrado. Orientador: Prof. Dr. Temístocles Cezar. Porto Alegre: UFRGS, IFCH - Departamento de História, Programa de Pós-Graduação em História, 2006, p.112.

40 FOUCAULT, Michel. *A arqueologia do saber*. Rio de Janeiro: Forense Universitária, 2009, p.31-32.

[. . .] Throughout the European nineteenth century, quite unique types of authors emerged, that cannot be confused with the "great" literary authors, nor the authors of canonical religious texts, nor with the founders of science. Let us call them then, somewhat arbitrarily, "Founders of Discursivity"(...) In contrast, when I speak of Marx and Freud as "founders of discourse", I mean that they not only made a number of analogies possible but also made (and how) a number of differences. They opened space for something different from them and which, however, belongs to what they have founded.[41]

Thus, whether we consider that *"founder of discursivity"* also operates a founding act by creating an *authority*, it is possible to apply the concept of *authority* established by Arendt to a modern historiographical culture.[42] "Because, after all, it is in fact ultimately about authority, more precisely enunciative authority, to distinguish it from the institutional authority" as Paul Ricœur synthesizes.[43]

Regarding the method to be used, I call upon the reflections of Michel Foucault present in *The Archaeology of Knowledge*. Considering that the annotation task of the *General History of Brazil* falls within a historiographical tradition, even if in formation, it enables annotators to mitigate the otherness characteristic of the foundational period of Brazilian historiography. Therefore, using Varnhagen's work to do so, the annotators have become the Viscount's heirs, thanks to the possibility of "isolating the innovations under a permanency

41 FOUCAULT, Michel. *O que é um autor?* Lisboa: Vega Editora, 1997, p.58-60.

42 According to Arendt, the concept of *authority* is likely to be thought of in other spheres of social life not only to the policy. In short, it is legitimate the concept of use arising from political philosophy to operationalize reflections linked to other spheres of social life, such as culture, for example. Arendt reminds us also that "the derivative character of authority and tradition in spiritual matters did not constitute impediment to them to become the prevalent traits in Western philosophical thought during most of our history." ARENDT, Hannah. *Que é Autoridade?* In: *Entre o passado e o futuro*. São Paulo: Perspectiva, 2007, p.167; Ver também: KOJÈVE, Alexandre. *La notion d'autorité*. Paris: Éditions Gallimard, 2004, p.117; REVAULT D'ALLONNES, Myriam. *El poder de los comienzos. Ensayo sobre la autoridad*. Buenos Aires: Amorrortu, 2008, p.68-71.

43 RICOEUR, Paul. *A memória, a história, o esquecimento*. Campinas: Editora da UNICAMP, 2007, p.74-75.

background and transferring its merit to the originality, the geniality, the very decision of individuals. "[44] For as long as this tradition is not interrupted, the founder's authority remains alive.[45] It will be important to consider the characteristics of Varnhagen's authority as the one who laid the foundation for the achievement of a potentially solid historiographical *project* in terms of disciplinary *heritage,* or tradition.[46]

Thus, I depart from the question of how the series of discourses articulated by Capistrano and Garcia during the annotation process of the *General History of Brazil* within this incipient historiographical tradition, enabled the mitigation of the otherness derived from the foundation of National History by said work. The otherness was reduced to the point of allowing corrections and criticisms on Viscount of Porto Seguro's book without deconstructing it, recognizing Varnhagen as an *authority* in the history of Brazil. The idea is to seek the moments of *discursive dispersion* experienced by the annotators, checking which *discursive strategies,* or which documents were privileged, which theoretical and methodological approaches remained, as well as examining whether the proposals suggested by Varnhagen about how Brazilian history should continue to be written, were followed by its annotators.[47] Because if it is possible to see this structural continuity

---

44 "This is the notion of tradition: it aims to give a unique temporal importance to a number of phenomena, while successive and identical (or at least similar); It allows us to rethink the dispersion of history in the form of this set; reduces the characteristic difference of any beginning, to back, without interruption, in the indefinite allocation of origin; thanks to it, the news can be isolated on a permanent fund, and merit transferred to the originality, the ingeniosity, the very decision of individuals. "FOUCAULT, Michel. *A arqueologia do saber*. Rio de Janeiro: Forense Universitária, 2009, p.23.
45 ARENDT, Hannah. *Que é Autoridade?* In: *Entre o passado e o futuro*. São Paulo: Perspectiva, 2007, p.166.
46 KOJÈVE, Alexandre. *La notion d'autorité*. Paris: Éditions Gallimard, 2004, p.67-68, 74, 85-88.
47 On these times when possible choices about a speech are presented to a speaker enunciating a certain discourse, Foucault wrote that: "But it is here to neutralize the discourse [. . .] but, on the contrary, keep it in its consistency, do so arise in the complexity of its own. In a word, we want to actually give up 'things', 'removing the present from their temporality'; [. . .] Replace the enigmatic treasure of 'things' speech prior to the regular formation of objects that only in it are outlined; define these *objects* without reference to the *bottom of things, but relating them to the set of rules that allow to train them as objects of a discourse and thus*

within national history writing process since Varnhagen until his annotators, then it is plausible to consider within the incipient tradition, a conforming process of the discourse on Brazilian History when it comes to Varnhagen's statements on the subject since the mid-nineteenth century to the mid-twentieth century.[48] Anyhow, Varnhagen's *authority* does not abolish the annotators' free will, it only restricts what is possible or not to choose and/or perform.[49]

However, it is important to note and comment a pioneer work within the study of footnotes that was certainly a great source of inspiration for this study. I refer to *The Footnote: A Curious History,* written by the American historian Anthony Grafton.[50] In his book, Grafton examines the advent of footnotes' technics within modern Western

---

constitute their historical appearance of conditions.(...) Finally, the enunciation field understands what might be called a memory area (these are the statements that are not even accepted or discussed, that do not define more, therefore, not a body of truths or a domain of validity, but for which they are established affiliation ties, genesis, transformation, continuity, and historical discontinuity). "FOUCAULT, Michel. *A arqueologia do saber.* Rio de Janeiro: Forense Universitária, 2009, p.54-55, 65.

48 Oliveira attests us in his note number 64, that the annotation work of Friar Vicente do Salvador, gives us the "example of the 'method' of source review as it was conceived and practiced by most Brazilian historians of the nineteenth century since at least Varnhagen. "OLIVEIRA, Maria da Glória. *Crítica, método e escrita da história em João Capistrano de Abreu (1853-1927).* Dissertação de Mestrado. Orientador: Prof. Dr. Temístocles Cezar. Porto Alegre: UFRGS, IFCH - Departamento de História, Programa de Pós-Graduação em História, 2006, p.105.

49 ARENDT, Hannah. *Que é Autoridade?* In: *Entre o passado e o futuro.* São Paulo: Perspectiva, 2007, p.133. Capistrano and Garcia for example, worked extensively to compile, record and criticize the sources and documents considered essential to the writing of the history of Brazil, "procedures taken in the nineteenth century as decisive for the disciplining of historical studies"; WEHLING, Arno. *Estado, história, memória: Varnhagen e a construção da identidade nacional.* Rio de Janeiro: Nova Fronteira, 1999, p.113-114; Some of these documents were discovered and first criticized by Varnhagen, such as the manuscripts of Gabriel Soares de Sousa, Martim Affonso, Fernão Cardim; Varnhagen also reissued the *Caramuru* and *Uruguay,* as well as printed or reprinted "rare or curious manuscripts," as the letter of Pero Vaz de Caminha; ABREU, J. Capistrano de. *Ensaios e estudos: (crítica e história).* 1. série. Rio de Janeiro: Sociedade Capistrano de Abreu, 1931, p.128-133; Segundo Ricoeur, é a "[. . .] existência de convenções que delimitam de antemão o campo dos possíveis [. . .]". RICOEUR, Paul. *A memória, a história, o esquecimento.* Campinas: Editora da UNICAMP, 2007, p.238.

50 GRAFTON, Anthony. *As origens trágicas da erudição: Pequeno tratado sobre a nota de rodapé.* Campinas: Papirus, 1998.

historiography from the seventeenth century to the present day, by analyzing more closely authors such as Ranke, whose work, for example, recognized as a landmark of the emergence of historiography considered scientific and whose notes allowed a broader substantiation of the narrative showing the sources used, as well as the "debates" and the "controversy" between the author and the bibliography used. According to Grafton, the prominence and the preference for the use of primary sources, for the exhausting work of tracking documents in the archives, involved the need for more rigorous review of sources to be cited or referenced in the footnotes. Moreover, the author notes that the preference for the primary documents would be related to the idea that the information obtained from these would be "direct", more "genuine" than other sources of information. Grafton also emphasizes the importance of the ecclesiastical exegesis documentary tradition and of scholarly practices of Renaissance antiquarians.

Finally, I believe it is important to discuss how the following chapters will be structured. The first chapter of this study will focus on the source from which the authority attributed to Varnhagen by his annotators in relation to the history of Brazil ultimately emanates. The function of the wide range of unpublished historical documents used latterly published by the Viscount de Porto Seguro will receive special attention. Those documents were rectified and validated critically, while Capistrano de Abreu and Rodolfo Garcia added others through the annotation process of the *General History of Brazil*. It will be argued that the great value attributed to these sources demonstrates a certain conception of history strictly guided by the belief in a sort of history whose existence is supposed to be guaranteed beyond the historiographical representations constructed about certain past realities. This enabled the notion that the history of Brazil, in order to be more complete, less lacunar, depended primarily on the collection and review of the sources. It is important to describe the limits of such historic discourse, which will lead us to the next chapter.

In a second moment, by reflecting on the footnotes of the *General History of Brazil*, I will deal with the specific case of a commemorative collection of books, some sort of "monument", used by Capistrano de Abreu and Rodolfo Garcia, but that was not crafted by Varnhagen since it was published only in 1922, the occasion of the celebrations of the first centenary of Brazilian independence. I refer to the *History of Portuguese Colonization in Brazil*, edited by Carlos Malheiro Dias and Albino Sousa Cruz and written by many colla-borators, among which we find Jaime Cortesão and Oliveira Lima. In the *History of Portuguese Colonization in Brazil* footnotes, as well as in the notes to the *General History of Brazil*, we noted the shaping phenomenon of Varnhagen's discursive authority regarding "National History" specifically due to the appreciation that both works have on the guiding perspective of history and its epistemological assump-tions. Even after almost a century, from 1854 to 1922, the *General History of Brazil* by Varnhagen still largely determining how Brazilian History should be written, especially the history of the colonial past.

Finally, after further considerations on the concept and pheno-menon of authority, I will consider how the discursive phenomenon of instituting Varnhagen authority's regarding the history of Brazil, that is, as a founder of historiography of his "Fatherland's History", was closely linked to the problems discussed in previous chapters. In other words, I will discuss the issue of how the conception history at the time was supported by a specific substrate of beliefs capable of emanating a potential authority, specifically through a set of pri-mary documents raised for writing a certain type of story, as well as the adoption of a strictly national guiding perspective; and how these elements allowed the institution of Francisco Adolfo de Varnhagen's authority, with consequent consolidation of conceptions of history and historiography recorded in his *General History of Brazil*, especially considering the process of disciplinary discursive formation of the his-tory of Brazil, then under construction.

Settling the bricks: Amongst *Artifices* and *Auctoritates*

For there to be an authority, first, there must be a social relationship, and that one element of this relationship recognizes the other's potential for action without reacting radically or denying said potential. An authority is always a temporal and historical phenomenon, which is structurally the same in essence although, only exists due to its temporal-historical subjects and structures.[51] Therefore, in order to the phenomenon of authority may occur the existence of a hierarchical structure among the subjects of social relations that cause this phenomenon is necessary, since what the parties of an authoritarian relationship have in common is precisely this hierarchy. Thus, the highest element, the subject that occupies the apex of the hierarchy, has the authority and exercises it in relation to other subjects hierarchically and sequentially underneath. However, an authority is always founded on the grounds of an external source emanating potential authority, which is not necessarily included in the social relationship of the hierarchy of authority between subjects. The source of authority is therefore always an external element to the hierarchy of authority relationship.[52]

So this first chapter will focus on the source from which the authority of the man who occupied the apex of the hierarchy that conformed one historical and historiographical tradition phenomenon ultimately emanates, from the mid-nineteenth century on: Varnhagen. Once such authority has been recognized by its annotators, both in textual-discursive sets and within the very composition of the *General History* through their footnotes and final sections, it is important to show how there were certain discursive conditions that allowed this authority to be fundamentally recognized because of the extreme value of said external focus, that is, in this case, the historical sources used for the writing of the *General History of Brazil*. The function

---

51 Kojève, Alexandre. La *notion d'autorité. Paris: Éditions* Gallimard, 2004, p.57-65, 118-120.
52 ARENDT, Hannah. *Que é Autoridade?* In: *Entre o passado e o futuro.* São Paulo: Perspectiva, 2007, p.135.

of the wide range of unpublished historical documents used by the Viscount de Porto Seguro will be especially discussed, which were rectified and validated critically, while others were added by Capistrano de Abreu and Rodolfo Garcia, through the work of such annotation process. Through the investigation of the footnotes records we realize how important the large volume of historical documents found and their respective use by Varnhagen opened ways to his recognition as the major authority on Brazilian history and historiography. These documents were, in the case here reported, the external focus from which the potential authority emanated.

The source of authority

Due to the death of Francisco Adolfo de Varnhagen on July 29, 1878, João Capistrano de Abreu published in 1878 an article called *Necrology of Francisco Adolfo de Varnhagen, Viscount of Porto Seguro*. In 1882, just a few years after his *Necrology* on Varnhagen, Capistrano published another text, entitled *On the Viscount of Porto Seguro*. Such important Capistrano's articles have already proven much of his conception about how should be written the Brazilian national history.[53]

> To think the constitution of the nation and to design the conditions for the writing of its history, therefore, are inseparable terms of the same transaction whose brands can be found in the essays written by Capistrano on the final decades of the nineteenth century. In some of them, we see how, under the pretext of commenting and reviewing recently published historical works, the historian circumscribes attributes of his office and, with them, points out some boundaries - then in demarcating process - of their discipline.[54]

---

53 OLIVEIRA, Maria da Glória. *Crítica, método e escrita da história em João Capistrano de Abreu (1853-1927)*. Dissertação de Mestrado. Orientador: Prof. Dr. Temístocles Cezar. Porto Alegre: UFRGS, IFCH - Departamento de História, Programa de Pós-Graduação em História, 2006, p.42.

54 OLIVEIRA, Maria da Glória. *Crítica, método e escrita da história em João Capistrano de Abreu (1853-1927)*. Dissertação de Mestrado. Orientador: Prof. Dr. Temístocles Cezar. Porto Alegre: UFRGS, IFCH - Departamento de História, Programa de Pós-Graduação em História, 2006, p.47.

Throughout these articles written at the end of the nineteenth century, Capistrano discussed the contributions of authors and works related to the Brazilian history and historiography, such as Varnhagen and João Francisco Lisboa.[55] As stated earlier, such articles presented a critique of the guiding perspective, their critical-historical method, theoretical conceptions, the sources used, and a short exposure of the path of historical studies in the country by then, not missing a discussion of the differences between these works and authors. This way, Capistrano outlined the main elements of what he believed to be the best way to write "National History", whose basic level consisted in the tracking and verification of the documents considered by the author as fundamental. Besides, it was necessary to indicate the gaps and discuss the facts previously narrated by their predecessors, specifically those narrated by Varnhagen. Finally, Capistrano believed to be necessary to note the relevant literature as well as the documents relating to the history of Brazil, especially those close to the period related to the colonial past.[56] Capistrano also argued that the narrative of "National History" was guided by "the body of creative doctrines that in recent years were constituted in science under the name of sociology." According to the author, ignorance of such theories would have been one of the great mistakes made by the author of the *General History of Brazil.*[57] From these concepts, Capistrano stated his historiographical project.

Moreover, Capistrano fully recognized the merits of Varnhagen, he considered that after the publication of his *General History* there was no one else able to present, in the emblematic expression formulated by Capistrano, such "Cyclopean mass of materials". Ca-

---

55 ABREU, J. Capistrano de. *Ensaios e estudos: (crítica e história).* 1. série. Rio de Janeiro: Sociedade Capistrano de Abreu, 1931, p.138-139, 214-215; OLIVEI-RA, Maria da Glória. *Crítica, método e escrita da história em João Capistrano de Abreu (1853-1927).* Dissertação de Mestrado. Orientador: Prof. Dr. Temístocles Cezar. Porto Alegre: UFRGS, IFCH - Departamento de História, Programa de Pós-Graduação em História, 2006, p.67.

56 OLIVEIRA, Maria da Glória. *Crítica, método e escrita da história em João Capistrano de Abreu (1853-1927).* Dissertação de Mestrado. Orientador: Prof. Dr. Temístocles Cezar. Porto Alegre: UFRGS, IFCH - Departamento de História, Programa de Pós-Graduação em História, 2006, p.104-105.

57 ABREU, J. Capistrano de. *Ensaios e estudos: (crítica e história).* 1. série. Rio de Janeiro: Sociedade Capistrano de Abreu, 1931, p.139.

pistrano also stressed that it would have been Varnhagen who first and most appropriately placed himself "under the actual national point of view" to build the narrative of national history.[58] Varnhagen's *General History of Brazil* represented therefore, according to Capistrano, the founding event of the Brazilian historiography.[59] Also according to the historian, the large set of primary sources discovered and accumulated by Varnhagen as well as the "national perspective" were the two main foundational cornerstones of Brazilian history and historiography.

After established the foundations of "National History" the construction continued along the baseboards.[60] Capistrano, like Garcia, believed that writing another general history of Brazil would require it to be "more complete than its predecessors," collecting and criticizing new documents and studies in order to better elucidate the spaces, the gaps in Brazilian historiography, such as the sixteenth-century ones and the issue of the *Flags*. The *Flags* were a specific

---

58 ABREU, J. Capistrano de. *Ensaios e estudos: (crítica e história)*. 1. série. Rio de Janeiro: Sociedade Capistrano de Abreu, 1931, p.135, 139; According to the historian Arno Wehling, Varnhagen "also avoided the 'provincialism solvent', because this would fragment the nation's cultural and political achievements in incomplete smaller units. For him, as for Martius, the historian should write the national unitary point of view, which was justified by political and ideological factors of his situation, but it could also be intellectually justified by the inconsistency of an excessively particularistic cultural *ethos*, frequent argument of nationalists of the nineteenth century against proviscialists."WEHLING, Arno. *Estado, história, memória: Varnhagen e a construção da identidade nacional*. Rio de Janeiro: Nova Fronteira, 1999, p.77.

59 OLIVEIRA, Maria da Glória. *Crítica, método e escrita da história em João Capistrano de Abreu (1853-1927)*. Dissertação de Mestrado. Orientador: Prof. Dr. Temístocles Cezar. Porto Alegre: UFRGS, IFCH - Departamento de História, Programa de Pós-Graduação em História, 2006, p.72.

60 According to the Brazilian Portuguese grammar and vocabulary the footnotes of a book are called *notas de rodapé*, which could be literally translated as *notes on baseboards*. Therefore, it is quite elucidative to think about footnotes as notes on boards at the base of book's page. "[. . .] In his critique of Varnhagen, Capistrano formulated the guidelines of a historiographical project. Therefore, it was essential to continue 'building' what started with the work of the Viscount de Porto Seguro, through documentary research and monographic OLIVEIRA, Maria da Glória. *Crítica, método e escrita da história em João Capistrano de Abreu (1853-1927)*. Dissertação de Mestrado. Orientador: Prof. Dr. Temístocles Cezar. Porto Alegre: UFRGS, IFCH - Departamento de História, Programa de Pós-Graduação em História, 2006, p.72.

kind of movement called upon by those dwellers labeled *bandeirantes* – Portuguese expression for "flag men" – in order to acquire wealth by making hostages of American Natives and trying to gather treasures like gold, silver, diamonds, emeralds or drugs. As Capistrano himself stated, this would be a progressive task to be bequeathed to future historians once "between the young people studying, is it possible that no one ambitions to make some obscure point in the past known? There are plenty of them, and each more important than the other."[61] Thus, historians of future generations should clarify such "dark spots of the past" by collecting and reviewing new documents and evaluating previous works and producing monographs on the history of Brazil.

However, in another way, the critical annotation work of the major Varnhagen's book by Capistrano and Garcia seemed to want to close the gaps not only of the history written by the Viscount of Porto Seguro, but also seemed to aim to complement the gaps of a history of Brazil beyond the pages and footnotes of the *General History of Brazil*. The *General History* was the foundational basis of the history and historiography of Brazil. A past and a history whose existence, according to the discourse enunciated by Capistrano and Garcia seemed to be guaranteed beyond the existence of its written representation.

According to the "dominant spirit in the historiography of the time", the documentary research and critical reviews of historiography especially served the purpose of better evidencing the national history. Such critical reviews fundamentally aimed the discovery of new documents, which might or might not corroborate such interpretations.[62] In the case of Varnhagen we can claim that there was basically rectification his work for the purpose of consolidation of the National monument that was his book. The document, duly analyzed and evaluated through the document review process so dear to the nineteenth and early twentieth century Brazilian historians, was

61 ABREU, J. Capistrano de. *Ensaios e estudos: (crítica e história)*. 1. série. Rio de Janeiro: Sociedade Capistrano de Abreu, 1931, p.199, 204-205.

62 WEHLING, Arno. *Estado, história, memória: Varnhagen e a construção da identidade nacional*. Rio de Janeiro: Nova Fronteira, 1999, p.139; as Varnhagen stated in his *general history of Brazil*, "Tradition, in harmony with some documents, makes us believe. "VARNHAGEN, Francisco Adolfo de. *História geral do Brasil: antes da sua separação e independência de Portugal*. 4.ed. integral. São Paulo: Melhoramentos, 1948-1953, p.307.

the central object in the cognitive phenomenon of constructing by representation a determined past reality. The sources were believed to have the supreme properties to testify as well as to certify a historical fact, as if the cognitive work done by the historian was a minor part in such an intellectual process. Therefore it would suffice to collect and collate multiple documents so that, recomposing the facts of the past in a succession believed correct, it would be possible to light up the history to the present spirits.

> Thus, there would be a full correlation between the ontologically preexisting historical reality and the product of the combination of the sources. Their possible limitations would be due to information deficiencies: for times or situations with little documentation, conclusions could be only approximate. [63]

However, talking about filling the gaps of history largely implies the belief in the existence of a history and a past that would exist beyond representations that human beings create about such realities. If we believe that history does not effectively exist beyond our representations how do we think that there might exist gaps that must necessarily be searched, found, and filled? Who determines where they are and what are the areas of the gaps? Why think about filling gaps in history if we believe that history does not exist effectively beyond our representations? If it is imperative that such gaps should be filled, it is because it is believed that a past framed in history would exist beyond the narratives and representations that we build about this past; and therefore would be necessary that historians turned the past cognizable, once it was supposed that this past was still veiled by such historical gaps; as if history did not depend fundamentally on the existence of the historian and his questions to exist.[64] Speech-discou-

---

63 WEHLING, Arno. *Estado, história, memória: Varnhagen e a construção da identidade nacional.* Rio de Janeiro: Nova Fronteira, 1999, p.142.

64 In any case, we can consider that all historical knowledge possess metaphorically such "incomplete" nature since every historical narrative is always a story about something that we can still learn about a specific object, and not a mere representation of an existing phenomenological structure beyond their own representations. About this lacunar character of history, Paul Veyne wrote that "the most curious is that the gaps of history spontaneously close our eyes and we only discern with effort, both are vague ideas about what we should *initially* expect

rse is not just a contact surface between a pre-existing reality and a language translation potentially more or less appropriate, but defines the very conditions for the objects of knowledge to be constructed and discursively articulated.

> [. . .] The object does not wait in limbo the order that will release it and allow it to incarnate in a visible and voluble objectivity; it does not pre-exist itself, retained by an obstruction to the first contours of light, but it exists under conditions of a complex relationship beam.[65]

According to Koselleck, "language and history remain dependent on each other, but never get to fully coincide."[66] It is precisely this interdependence between language and history that is the bundle of discursive relations that determine and enable the creation of discourses and its objects. Such determinant relations of discourse and its objects are always historical, being related largely to institutions and norms, political, social, and economic processes. These relationships, precisely because they are historical, do not exist intrinsically to the objects from which speeches were articulated, but they conform the conditions of possibility for the emergence of a group of specific statements at certain times.[67] The past to be historicized is not an obvious reality. History is a discipline that requires the construction of its objects and methods to respond to certain historical issues, in other words, it is a discipline built on arguments and on an active construction process of past realities about which historians construct their representations of the past.[68] The document found in the archive is

---

to find in history, when we approach devoid of an elaborate questionnaire. A century is a white in our sources, and evil reader feels the gap. The historian can devote ten pages to a single day and compress ten years in two lines. "VEYNE, Paul. *Como se escreve a história; Foucault revoluciona a história*. Brasília: Editora UNB, 2008, p.26-27.

65 FOUCAULT, Michel. *A arqueologia do saber*. Rio de Janeiro: Forense Universitária, 2009, p.50.

66 KOSELLECK, Reinhart. *Futuro Passado, Contribuição à semântica dos tempos históricos*. Rio de Janeiro: Contraponto/Ed.PUCRJ, 2006, p.267.

67 FOUCAULT, Michel. *A arqueologia do saber*. Rio de Janeiro: Forense Universitária, 2009, p.50.

68 GUMBRECHT, Hans Ulrich. *As funções da retórica parlamentar na Revolução*

not necessarily a thing of the past, but a possible trace. If such an object persisted and is still present, how can it be part of the past? In this sense the Past is first of all a quality, an adjective.[69] The very choice of the documents is already intrinsically a moment of reality construction and displacement of an object from its place in the world from a first set of space-time coordinates, to some other posterior order.[70]

In the nineteenth century, modern history has become its own subject. Intending to become a coherent totality, it began to have an effective and processual reality content as they had not existed before. It went on to frame the events of the histories so far considered individual ones, becoming a huge generalized process, whose writing and discipline no longer would specifically differ under the name of history. "Formulated in a concise way, the 'history' was a kind of transcendent category that pointed to the condition of possibility of histories."[71] Thus, regarding the referred Brazilian case, I believe historians hoped to define the Nation according to historical contours, so it was possible to grant it "an identity in the broader set of 'Nations', according to the new organizing principles of social life in the nineteenth century."[72] Therefore, the colonial history took an important role in shaping the colonial past of Portuguese America as specifically Brazilian past and history.

Varnhagen wrote his history subscribing Brazil to the progressive temporal and collective process conceived as the history of mankind, especially from the focus of the pioneer European maritime expansion, the Portuguese one, and the consequent process of colonization

---

Francesa: estudos preliminares para uma pragmática histórica do texto. Belo Horizonte: Editora UFMG, 2003, p.23-25.

69 PROST, Antoine. *Doze lições sobre a história.* Belo Horizonte: Autêntica Editora, 2008, p.64.

70 CERTEAU, Michel de. *A escrita da história.* Rio de Janeiro: Forense Universitária, 2006, p.81-82.

71 KOSELLECK, Reinhart. *historia/Historia.* Madri: Editorial Trotta, 2004, p.32, 37, 39, 45; Ver também: ARENDT, Hannah. *O Conceito de História – Antigo e Moderno* In: *Entre o passado e o futuro.* São Paulo: Perspectiva, 2007, p.69-126.

72 GUIMARÃES, Manoel Luiz Salgado. Nação e civilização nos trópicos: o Instituto Histórico e Geográfico Brasileiro e o projeto de uma História Nacional. *Estudos Históricos,* Rio de Janeiro, n.1, p.5-27, 1988, p.6.

of the new lands.[73] Martius had previously proposed such a history to Brazil.[74] To Varnhagen, and certainly for many of his contemporaries, it was as if the Ourique Miracle of July 25, 1139, extended a sacred monarchical aura until September 7, 1822, blessing the birth of the awaited Empire, gestated after three centuries of colonial history.[75] Thus, the Viscount of Porto Seguro built his *General History* according to the conception that "Brazil is whole, one, [and] independent by the grace of the Braganza House", which is why the "big theme of his book is the work of Portuguese colonization in Brazil."[76] It is not by chance that his greatest work is entitled *General History of Brazil: before its separation and independence of Portugal.* Or, as stated by Manuel Salgado Guimarães about Varnhagen's *History* and about the historiography designed by the scholars of the Brazilian Geographical and Historical Institute (BHGI) during the nineteenth century:

> Against a backdrop of exuberant nature, the accomplishments of Lusitanian ancestors should inspire the work of laying the monarchy in the tropics, solidifying the monarchical principles as a form of government and ensuring the continuity of the Braganza house. (...) In the case of the Brazilian Empire, founded in 1822, and the first generation of literati gathered around the BHGI and the publication of its quarterly magazine project, it would be the demands

73 MATTOS, Selma Rinaldi de. *O Brasil em lições: a história como disciplina escolar em Joaquim Manuel de Macedo.* Rio de Janeiro: Access, 2000, p.106-107.

74 "Considering the history of mankind 'in the middle of its top development', Martius proposes the objective of a Brazilian historian to enter the country's history in the process, since the country is in 'progressive development', as attested by the mixing of populations." WEHLING, Arno. *Estado, história, memória: Varnhagen e a construção da identidade nacional.* Rio de Janeiro: Nova Fronteira, 1999, p.41.

75 RODRIGUES, José Honório. *História da História do Brasil.* São Paulo: Companhia Editora Nacional, 1978-1988, p.6-8.

76 RODRIGUES, José Honório. *História da História do Brasil.* São Paulo: Companhia Editora Nacional, 1978-1988, p.13-17; "Jose Honorio Rodrigues has recorded the fact that the great theme of Varnhagen was the colonizing work of Portugal in Brazil, while Américo Jacobina Lacombe highlighted the support given to the Portuguese colonization. The underlying reason is evident in the work and correspondence of Varnhagen, it was to value the dominance of Portuguese origin over blacks and indigenous, a sensitive issue at a time of large influx of African labor, and in which current anti-lusitanian highlighted the indigenous role in colonization ". WEHLING, Arno. *Estado, história, memória: Varnhagen e a construção da identidade nacional.* Rio de Janeiro: Nova Fronteira, 1999, p.187.

arising from the need to found a nation in the former Portuguese colonial space that would make revisiting the past a demand, in order to ensure a future project.[77]

So the idea of a Brazil nationally and territorially unified in the nineteenth century conditioned historians to see the history of the former Portuguese colonies in America as the history of the future Brazilian national state, in order to collaborate with the process of state consolidation and national formation, which they contemporaneously experienced and motivated while members of the dominant social group. "In the work of Varnhagen, the actors and the social dynamics converge to a teleological point that is the Brazilian formation."[78]

However, this does not mean that it was strictly about psychological or conscious motivations of the authors in question, but the historical conditions for the creation of a subject and a speech object about which it was possible to state certain group of speeches.[79]

> [...] The strategic choices do not emerge directly from a worldview or a predominance of interests that belongs to this or that speaking subject; but its very possibility [of existence] is divergently determined by the playing of concepts [...].[80]

In the specific case of *General History* of *Brazil,* those footnotes written by Capistrano and Garcia allow us to look at how the choices made by them during the critical annotation work of the Viscount's great book cooperated to this process of consolidation of the idea of a unified Brazilian Nation by reaffirming the theoretical and epistemological structure of Varnhagen's "iron frames". Most primary sour-

---

77 GUIMARÃES, Manoel Luiz Salgado.*Entre as Luzes e o Romantismo: as tensões da escrita da história no Brasil oitocentista.* In:GUIMARÃES, Manoel Luiz Salgado (Org.).*Estudos sobre a escrita da história.* Rio de Janeiro: 7Letras, 2006, p.75, 83.
78 WEHLING, Arno. *Estado, história, memória: Varnhagen e a construção da identidade nacional.* Rio de Janeiro: Nova Fronteira, 1999, p.186; Ver também: MATTOS, Ilmar Rohloff de. *O tempo Saquarema.* São Paulo: HUCITEC; [Brasília, DF]: INL, 1987.
79 FOUCAULT, Michel. *A arqueologia do saber.* Rio de Janeiro: Forense Universitária, 2009, p.66, 76-77.
80 FOUCAULT, Michel. *A arqueologia do saber.* Rio de Janeiro: Forense Universitária, 2009, p.81.

ces discovered and utilized by Varnhagen during the *General History's* composition were also noted and subsequently studied by Capistrano Abreu and / or Rodolfo Garcia.[81] The huge range of documents collected by the Viscount seemed to emanate a possibility of direct access to the past, or as it was believed, history. So, recasting the so dear conception held by historians since at least the late nineteenth century, that the primary sources would enable more direct access to the past; I may think that the documents accumulated by Varnhagen served as a set of *indices of preterit realities.*[82]

As stated by the North-American logical-analytic philosopher Charles Sanders Peirce, an *index* is a modulation of a sign, and a sign is one thing that leads to another thing to refer to an object that can be identified to it, as well as the real conception we have of an object is a sign that connects the idea we have of this object to the object itself. The modulation of a sign into an *index* takes the sign to establish a relationship as direct as possible, even the spatial one, with the object of reference, as well as with the senses and the memory of the person to whom the sign serves as an index.[83] Regarding the objects of interest to the potential discipline of history, an object like a very old building, like a listed building for some heritage institution, for example, could serve as an *index* of a past reality, as one may think that such building is the closest point possible to get direct access to the past. However, as previously stated, the past is above all a quality, not an effective reality that exists beyond the cognitive relations and representations that we have of a past reality whatsoever. Thus, because object-documents would have persisted from a determined past reality until some equally specific present time, they would supposedly have the power to connect, as directly as possible, the mind of a cognizant subject (the historian and/or its

---

81 GARCIA, Rodolfo. *Sistemas de classificação bibliográfica: da classificação decimal e suas vantagens.* Rio de Janeiro: Associação Brasileira de Bibliotecários, 1969, p.3-9; WEHLING, Arno. *Estado, história, memória: Varnhagen e a construção da identidade nacional.* Rio de Janeiro: Nova Fronteira, 1999, p.137-139, 153.

82 On the belief that the primary sources would allow more direct access to the past, see: GRAFTON, Anthony. *As origens trágicas da erudição: Pequeno tratado sobre a nota de rodapé.* Campinas: Papirus, 1998, p.55; e HARTOG, François. *Évidence de l'histoire. Ce que voient les historiens.* Paris: Gallimard/Éditions de EHESS, 2005.

83 PEIRCE, Charles Sanders. *Semiótica.* São Paulo: Perspectiva, 2003, p.74.

partners) and the past reality from which those objects are derived. For sure these relations are not absolute, rather dependent on the relation between the objects, documents and the mind of the knower.[84]

In this sense, Paul Veyne argued that "the historical narrative lies beyond all documents, since none of them could be the event itself; it is not a documentary photomontage and it does not show the past to the living 'as if they were there.' "The documents and its consequent narrative representation does not allow us, by reason of their specific nature, that kind of potentially direct access to the past, because "history is nothing but answers to our questions," conditioned by the interest of the historian, by the conservational status of the documentation or "how much more" may interfere in the relationship between the knowing mind and the object of analysis.[85]

However, for the historians involved in this study, it seemed very important to collect and criticize the largest possible number of documents on colonial history, it was believed that the more documents – which would allow the historian such direct access to the past making his storytelling as gap free as possible - more true and complete story would be told in relation to the desired past. Those are the reasons why I believe Varnhagen specifically appreciated the colonial sources to define his conception of Brazilian history and nation, as also did their annotators and critics. In the said set of modern nations, it seemed necessary to define clearly, without flaws or gaps, the history and identity of a nation.

> Varnhagen's interpretations were grounded almost always by 'discoveries', in other words, by ignored documentary lodes or forgotten ones by his predecessors. The 'fear of the unprecedented' extremely strong in historicist historiography, supposed intimacy with archival sources, understood as a sure sign to the right information and the scope of historical truth; underlying this bias found itself the supposed idealist an immutable pre-existing reality, waiting for its correct identification by the subject.
>
> The affirmation of the scientific history within an intellectual context of knowledge with increasingly well-defined boundaries passed thus necessarily by the establishment of a documentary *corpus,* from which the historical knowledge would be built, once all other

84 PEIRCE, Charles Sanders. *Semiótica*. São Paulo: Perspectiva, 2003, p.64-70.
85 VEYNE, Paul. *Como se escreve a história; Foucault revoluciona a história*. Brasília: Editora UNB, 2008, p.18, 36-37.

options - the philosophy of history, historical fiction, rhetoric, chronic and Maurinian erudition - were only imperfect approximations of this unique phenomenon that the documentation revealed.[86]

Such "worship" of the document was therefore a first step in the process of constituting a national memory and "National History". Along the *General History of Brazil* and its respective mass of documents, the possibility of narrating colonial history according the "actual national point of view" was guaranteed, in other words, a process whose culmination was then the Second Empire. As Capistrano de Abreu once stated, "Varnhagen serves only to Brazil."[87]

Once the foundations for the construction and dissemination of Varnhagen's frame for national history were laid - whose outstanding elements hitherto were: a history with potential existence beyond representations; primacy of primary documents and national *guiding perspective* - remained to Capistrano de Abreu and Rodolfo Garcia, the roles of advocates of Varnhagen's great historical narrative about Brazil. Throughout the *General History of Brazil*'s footnotes we can see moments of *discursive dispersion* in which the limits and the conditions of existence of statements about the history of Brazil were defined, from at least 1854 until the mid-twentieth century. This does not mean that there was no gradual change in the discursive formation in question, and that alternative statements were not able to flourish, but that this great speech proved to be crucial and determinant of other sets of statements about the history of Brazil, which allows us to think of a discursive consolidation of Varnhagen's authority as the founder of national history. This process is observable and supported by the annotation of his *General History*, once in these notes are found, in a privileged way, the records of the recognition of Viscount of Porto Seguro's authority. In this process, the authors or sources that went to meet the center argumentative and plotting line proposed by Varnhagen were more valued and privileged to write such footnotes.[88]

---

86 WEHLING, Arno. *Estado, história, memória: Varnhagen e a construção da identidade nacional.* Rio de Janeiro: Nova Fronteira, 1999, p.153, 193.
87 ABREU, J. Capistrano de. *Ensaios e estudos: (crítica e história).* 1. série. Rio de Janeiro: Sociedade Capistrano de Abreu, 1931, p.139.
88 On these times, when possible choices about a speech are presented in relation

The documents and the colonial past

Varnhagen died in Vienna on July 29, 1878, at the age of 62, shortly after the publication of the second edition of his *General History of Brazil.* [89] Later, the historians João Capistrano de Abreu and Rodolfo Garcia took upon themselves the fearful and long task of annotating the then masterpiece of Brazilian historiography. To carry out this complex task, Capistrano and Garcia had, besides the numerous works that Varnhagen discovered, collected, criticized and edited, many others which had not been made public during the life of the Viscount. In scholarly notes written and added by the two annotators to the *General History of Brazil,* we can see references and citations of unpublished monographs, newly discovered documents and multiple issues of the *Journal of the Brazilian Historical and Geographical Institute,* as well as volumes such as the *Annaes of the National Library,* dated from 1876, and the volumes of the *First Visitation of the Holy Office.* [90]

This last set of texts was prefaced by Capistrano and Rodolfo Garcia and initially published by the Capistrano de Abreu Society

---

to a particular set of discursive, Foucault wrote that: "But it is here to neutralize the discourse [...] but, on the contrary, keep it in its consistency, do so arise in the complexity of its own. In a word, we want to actually give up 'things', removing the present from their temporality; [...] Replace the enigmatic treasure of 'things' speech prior to the regular formation of objects that only in it are outlined; define these *objects* without reference to the *bottom of things, but relating them to the set of rules that allow them as objects of a discourse and thus constitute their historical appearance of conditions.(...) Finally, the enunciation field understands what might be called a memory area (these are the statements that are not even accepted or discussed, that do not define more, therefore, not a body of truths or a domain of validity, but for which they are established affiliation ties, genesis, transformation, continuity, and historical discontinuity).* "FOUCAULT, Michel. *A arqueologia do saber.* Rio de Janeiro: Forense Universitária, 2009, p.53-54, 64.

89 CEZAR, Temístocles. Varnhagen em movimento: breve antologia de uma existência. *Topoi: Revista de História,* Rio de Janeiro: Programa de Pós-graduação em História Social da UFRJ / 7Letras, v.8, n.15, p. 159-207, jul.-dez., 2007, p.186.

90 "The Institute [Capistrano de Abreu] always highlighted the zeal from its founders in the collection and organization of interesting documents to national history, much of which were transcribed in the pages of its trimestral magazine ".MATTOS, Ilmar Rohloff de. *Capítulos de Capistrano.* In: *Modernos Descobrimentos do Brasil.* http://www.historiaecultura.pro.br/modernosdescobrimentos/desc/capistrano/frame.htm.Accessed on 19/09/2010.

in 1922, within the "Eduardo Prado Series".[91] The analysis of these works offers us some important elements to develop the reflection on the discursive conformation of Varnhagen's authority on the history of Brazil through the annotation of the *General History.* We start, therefore, with the analysis of the *Preface* written by Capistrano de Abreu in addition to the *First Visitation of the Holy Office to parts of Brazil by the licensee Heitor Furtado Mendoça: Confessions of Bahia (1591-92).* In his *Preface,* Capistrano wrote not only about the general characteristics of the volume's content, commenting on some of the confessions, but also writing a brief history of the first visit of the institution to the Portuguese colony, speculating their motives.[92]

To compose the *Preface* mentioned above, in addition to numerous references to magazines, especially the Historical Portuguese Archive's ones, and *the Annaes of the National Library* Capistrano also used more recurrently the *Medieval heresy & the Inquisition* by Turberville and the *History of the New Christian Portugueses,* by his friend João Lúcio d'Azevedo.[93] However, what draws our attention to the *Preface* in question is the fact that a large number of historical information gathered from primary sources used by the author is related to the documents used by Varnhagen in his *General History,* or even by Capistrano de Abreu and Rodolfo Garcia to add footnotes to the Viscount's masterpiece. José de Anchieta, Nobrega, Gandavo, Fernão Cardim, Friar Vicente do Salvador and Gabriel Soares, although not having appeared in the footnotes, constantly appeared in the text to corroborate Capis-

---

91 MENDOÇA, Heitor Furtado de. *Primeira visitação do Santo Officio as partes do Brasil pelo licenciado Heitor Furtado de Mendoça: Confissões da Bahia (1591-1592).* Rio de Janeiro: F. Briguiet, 1935; _____. *Primeira visitação do Santo Officio ás partes do Brasil pelo licenciado Heitor Furtado de Mendoça: Denunciações da Bahia (1591-1593).* São Paulo: Ed. Paulo Prado, 1925; _____. *Primeira visitação do Santo Officio ás partes do Brasil pelo licenciado Heitor Furtado de Mendoça: Denunciações de Pernambuco (1593-1595).* São Paulo: Ed. Paulo Prado, 1929.

92 ABREU, J. C.. *Prefácio de J. Capistrano de Abreu.* In: MENDOÇA, Heitor Furtado de. *Primeira visitação do Santo Officio as partes do Brasil pelo licenciado Heitor Furtado de Mendoça: Confissões da Bahia (1591-1592).* Rio de Janeiro: F. Briguiet, 1935, p.I-XXIX.

93 ABREU, J. C.. *Prefácio de J. Capistrano de Abreu.* In: MENDOÇA, Heitor Furtado de. *Primeira visitação do Santo Officio as partes do Brasil pelo licenciado Heitor Furtado de Mendoça: Confissões da Bahia (1591-1592).* Rio de Janeiro: F. Briguiet, 1935,p.I-VI, VIII-IX, XIV, XVI, XVII, XIX, XXII-XXIX.

trano's narrative.[94] In *Denunciations of Bahia,* whose introduction was also written by Capistrano de Abreu, we find again as a reference to the composition of his brief text, the recurring names of Gabriel Soares de Souza, Fr. Jaboatão, Friar Vicente do Salvador, and Pero Magalhães de Gandavo.[95]. As previously stated, besides having been used to critically note the *General History of Brazil,* such sources were discovered and even collected, criticized and/or edited by Varnhagen. The Viscount himself was repeatedly used by Capistrano in the *Preface.*[96]

Regarding the usage of Varnhagen, it is important to note and consider a particular movement of Capistrano's speech on the "National History". The edition of the *General History of Brazil* used and cited by Capistrano in the critical study that gives body to the *Preface* of the *First Visitation of the Holy Office: Confessions of Bahia* is precisely the one that the historian himself was about to annotate and criticize. Whereas Capistrano's *Preface* is dated back to the "inaugural publication" in1922, and that his annotation of the *General History* had begun in 1906, being interrupted due to a fire in the printing house and resumed by Rodolfo Garcia in 1928, we can judge that critical studies of Capistrano on the colonial sources in question were executed concurrently to his annotation work on the third edition of the *General History of Brazil.*[97] The third annotated edition of this work, initiated

---

94 ABREU, J. C.. *Prefácio de J. Capistrano de Abreu.* In: MENDOÇA, Heitor Furtado de. *Primeira visitação do Santo Officio as partes do Brasil pelo licenciado Heitor Furtado de Mendoça: Confissões da Bahia (1591-1592).* Rio de Janeiro: F. Briguiet, 1935, p.I-VIII, XVIII, XXI.

95 ABREU, J. C.. *Prefácio de J. Capistrano de Abreu.* In: MENDOÇA, Heitor Furtado de. *Primeira visitação do Santo Officio as partes do Brasil pelo licenciado Heitor Furtado de Mendoça: Confissões da Bahia (1591-1592).* Rio de Janeiro: F. Briguiet, 1935,São Paulo: Ed Paulo Prado, 1925 p.11, 12, 14-17.

96 ABREU, J. C.. *Prefácio de J. Capistrano de Abreu.* In: MENDOÇA, Heitor Furtado de. *Primeira visitação do Santo Officio as partes do Brasil pelo licenciado Heitor Furtado de Mendoça: Confissões da Bahia (1591-1592).* Rio de Janeiro: F. Briguiet, 1935, p.III, VII, IX.

97 "Capistrano de Abreu began the publication of a third edition of the work, corrected and annotated by himself in 1906, but he did not finish because of a fire in the publishing house. Rodolfo Garcia took over the project in 1928 and published it in five volumes, the third complete edition, with his comments and Capistrano's work on the original text of Varnhagen. " CEZAR, Temístocles. *L'écriture de l'histoire au Brésil au XIXe siècle: essai sur une rhétorique de la nacionalité : Le cas Varnhagen.* Tese de Doutorado. Orientador: Prof. Dr. François Hartog. Paris: EHESS, 2002, p.540-541; ABREU, J. C.. *Prefácio de J. Capistrano*

by Capistrano and completed by Rodolfo Garcia precisely shows us in its footnotes and notes of final sections a great appreciation of the huge range of colonial documents used largely with primacy and originality by the Viscount.

Thus, *General History of Brazil* was placed as the fundamental baseline in relation to the writing of" National History": it was considered to be both a source to be used to write other histories, and the main and most complete narrative about the history of Brazil ever to be written until the first decades of the twentieth century. According to Capistrano and Garcia, the *History* by Varnhagen was indeed the main existing national historiographical narrative until then, precisely because of the extensive use of colonial documents and the adoption of a national guiding perspective that would bring the desired narrative meaning, a prospect that was then judged as the most appropriate.

Finally, regarding the series of documents related to the *First Visitation of the Holy Office to parts of Brazil,* we analyze Rodolfo Garcia's *Introduction* to the volume devoted to *the Denunciations of Pernambuco (1593-1595).*

Early on, Garcia made it clear that he would follow the path of Capistrano de Abreu, his "always remembered master". In the opening paragraphs of his *Introduction,* the author commented on some of activities related to the documentary research performed by Capistrano. According to Garcia, Capistrano had examined "the apographo of the *Life* of the venerable apostle of Brazil, written by Father Pero Rodrigues", present in Évora Library "and published later in the *Annaes of the National Library*, vol. XIX, 1897", and has subsequently worked with a more complete copy of said work, present in the Alcobaça fund of the National Library of Lisbon, which "was published in said *Annaes,* vol. XXIX, 1907, both editions containing his notes, which authenticate it". Capistrano possibly had access to such sources through the favors provided by his Portuguese friends such as João Lúcio de Azevedo and Antonio Baião, who sent him rare or newly discovered documents. Moreover, Capistrano has done the priest Antonio Vieira's biography, and "when death surprised him, he was preparing to comment, by request of Max Fleiuss for the Historical Institute, the

---

de Abreu. In: MENDOÇA, Heitor Furtado de. *Primeira visitação do Santo Officio as partes do Brasil pelo licenciado Heitor Furtado de Mendoça: Confissões da Bahia (1591-1592).* Rio de Janeiro: F. Briguiet, 1935, p.XXIX.

Epistolary Narrative of Fernão Cardim, a work that would be definiti-ve to the comprehension of this extraordinary Jesuit. "[98]

Thus, Garcia opened the convenient room to comment in a specific way, the two previous volumes of the series concerning the *First Visitation of the Holy Office.* According to the author, "On the first two volumes - *Confessions and Denunciations of Bahia,* São Paulo -Rio, 1922-1925, Capistrano de Abreu reported as much as possible about the visitor, his biography prior to the visit, his activities in the city of Salvador and at Recôncavo region.»[99]

Regarding the documents used to compose his introductory study to the *Denunciations of Pernambuco,* Rodolfo Garcia followed largely the footsteps of his "master" Capistrano. Among other refe-rences, we find some less recurrent ones in the introductory studies inserted in the documentary series of the *First Visitation of the Holy Office,* such as the *Manuelinas Ordinances,* the *Records of the Overseas Council,* the *Annaes of the National Library,* the *Journal of the History Institute* and the *Journal of the Archeological Institute of Pernambuco.*[100] However, between notes or within the body of the text of Garcia's *Introduction,* re-emerged references to some more persistent docu-ments already mentioned above. This is the case of the 1918 edition of *History of Brazil* by Friar Vicente do Salvador, of *New Brazilian Orb Seraphic* written in 1858 by Antônio de Santa Maria Jaboatão, and the writings by the Fathers Manuel da Nobrega, Anchieta as well as Fernão Cardim.[101]

---

98 GARCIA, Rodolfo. *Introducção.* In: MENDOÇA, Heitor Furtado de. *Primeira vi-sitação do Santo Officio ás partes do Brasil pelo licenciado Heitor Furtado de Mendoça: Denunciações de Pernambuco (1593-1595).* São Paulo: Ed. Paulo Prado, 1929, p..V-VII.

99 GARCIA, Rodolfo. *Introducção.* In: MENDOÇA, Heitor Furtado de. *Primeira visitação do Santo Officio ás partes do Brasil pelo licenciado Heitor Furtado de Men-doça: Denunciações de Pernambuco (1593-1595).* São Paulo: Ed. Paulo Prado, 1929, p..VII.

100 GARCIA, Rodolfo. *Introducção.* In: MENDOÇA, Heitor Furtado de. *Pri-meira visitação do Santo Officio ás partes do Brasil pelo licenciado Heitor Furtado de Mendoça: Denunciações de Pernambuco (1593-1595).* São Paulo: Ed. Paulo Prado, 1929, p.XIII, XV-XVI, XX, XXIII-XXIV, XXVI, XXXI; Sobre o *Instituto Archeologico e Geographico Pernambucano,* ver: SCHWARCZ, Lília Moritz. *O espetáculo das raças: cientistas, instituições e questão racial no Brasil: 1870-1930.* São Paulo: Companhia das Letras, 1993, p.117-125.

101 GARCIA, Rodolfo. *Introducção.* In: MENDOÇA, Heitor Furtado de. *Primeira visitação do Santo Officio ás partes do Brasil pelo licenciado Heitor Furtado de Men-*

The other parts of the *First Visitation of the Holy Office* series were also used in the composition of the introductory study produced by Rodolfo Garcia for *Denunciations of Pernambuco*. The *Denunciations of Bahia* appeared referenced sixteen times - without counting the times when they were cited for different reasons, as in the case in which Garcia explains the censorship on sexuality issues – making even usage of the *Introduction* composed by João Capistrano de Abreu. In addition, Garcia also cited the *"Pernambuco Confessions'* third book, still unpublished" and the fourth edition of Varnhagen's *General History of Brazil*, which was being critically noted by Rodolfo Garcia during 1929, same year when *Denunciations of Pernambuco* were published containing his own *Introduction*.[102]

Therefore, we can assume the studies of Capistrano and Garcia about the volumes of the *First Visitation of the Holy Office to parts of Brazil* were not detached from his studies for the annotation of Varnhagen's work and from colonial sources the Viscount had discovered, collected, criticized and published as the previously mentioned writings by José de Anchieta, Father Manuel da Nóbrega, Pero de Magalhães Gândavo, Fernão Cardim, Friar Vicente do Salvador and Gabriel Soares de Sousa. The possibilities to tell the story of Brazil without touching these authors were restricted and only began to raise when monographs and new studies were conducted as well as discovery of inedited sources.

The *Treatises of the land and people of Brazil* by Fernão Cardim, for example, was one of the colonial sources used by Varnhagen that most received attention from Capistrano and Garcia. In their critical edition of the *Treaties of the land and people of Brazil* they included

---

doça: *Denunciações de Pernambuco (1593-1595)*. São Paulo: Ed. Paulo Prado, 1929, p.VII, X-XII, XIV-XVII, XXIX-XXX.

102 "The sexual sins against nature are not so much these denunciations but the *confessions* and *denunciations of Bahia*, already published, and *Pernambuco Confessions, still unpublished. As rightly did Capistrano with regard to the former, they are here pointed out the places where the subject is addressed: infrastructure, 37/38, 49/50, 53, 279/281, 400/401, 437/438, 442/444, 463 / 464. With this index the rough steps can be avoided or sought, will the reader will.* "GARCIA, Rodolfo. *Introducção*. In: MENDOÇA, Heitor Furtado de. *Primeira visitação do Santo Ofício ás partes do Brasil pelo licenciado Heitor Furtado de Mendoça: Denunciações de Pernambuco (1593-1595)*. São Paulo: Ed. Paulo Prado, 1929, p.VIII, XII-XIV, XVI-XIX, XXIII, XXVIII-XXX, XXXIII.

not only notes, but also introductory texts and an appendix.[103] Once again we can observe the great valorization of texts and authors from the colonial period to the writing of the history of Brazil.

Originally, the *Treatises of the land and people of Brazil* by Fernão Cardim were made of three distinct volumes, recognized under the names of: *Of the Climate and the Land of Brazil, Of the Beginning and Origin of the Brazilian Indians,* and *Epistolary Narrative, or Information on the Mission of Father Christovão de Gouvêa to parts of Brazil.*[104] In 1923, under the auspices of Afrânio Peixoto, then President of the Brazilian Academy of Letters, there was an attempt to "start the publication of two series of rare and precious works," dealing with "national classics" of literature and history. These issues should also, in the words of Peixoto, be "enriched with bibliographical introduction, and explanatory notes, of which will be in charge our confreres who had penchant for this kind of study."[105]

The text that compounds *Of the Climate and Land of Brazil,* whose original manuscript could be found in Évora Library was produced by Senator Cândido Mendes from an existing codex in the Brazilian Historical and Geographical Institute and partly published by his son Fernando Mendes. In 1885, Capistrano de Abreu published a full version, recognizing that the manuscript of Évora Library coincided with the version published in English by Samuel Purchas in 1625. In 1601, the Jesuit Fernão Cardim was imprisoned by two ships of English privateers and reportedly had his manuscripts dispossessed by the British, which was later bought by the London collector Samuel Purchas.[106] The notes were under Rodolfo Garcia's responsibility. In Évora Library was also the manuscript of *the Beginning and Origin of the Brazilian Indians,* which had also been published by Purchas in 1625. Just as it has happened to *Of the Climate and Land of Brazil,* the second part of Cardim's work has also been identified and edited

103 CARDIM, Fernão. *Tratados da terra e gente do Brasil.* São Paulo: Companhia Editora Nacional, 1939.
104 GARCIA, Rodolfo. *Introducção Geral.* In: CARDIM, Fernão. *Tratados da terra e gente do Brasil.* São Paulo: Companhia Editora Nacional, 1939, *p.8.*
105 GARCIA, Rodolfo. *Introducção Geral.* In: CARDIM, Fernão. *Tratados da terra e gente do Brasil.* São Paulo: Companhia Editora Nacional, 1939, *p.7.*
106 GARCIA, Rodolfo. *Introducção Geral.* In: CARDIM, Fernão. *Tratados da terra e gente do Brasil.* São Paulo: Companhia Editora Nacional, 1939, *p.15.*

by Capistrano de Abreu, although this has occurred four years earlier, in 1881. The footnotes added to *Of the Beginning and Origin of the Brazilian Indians* were under the responsibility of Bapstista Caetano de Almeida Nogueira.[107]

The last part of the *Treaties of the land and people of Brazil*, entitled *Epistolary Narrative or Information on the Mission of Father Christovão de Gouvêa to parts of Brazil*, was also copied from a manuscript present in the Évora Library, but in this case, was Varnhagen who did it. In 1847, the Viscount copied and published in Lisbon an edition of the *Epistolary Narrative*, a work that had been widely used in the composition of the *General History of Brazil*. According to Peixoto Rodolfo Garcia should be in charge of the footnotes to be attached to the *Epistolary Narrative*, once "not Varnhagen then, or later, Eduardo Prado's edition of the Historical Institute, 1902, could give it the necessary notes." In his words, Peixoto still placed Fernão Cardim as a "link of this chain to which belonged Anchieta and Vieira," as someone who established, between the two of them, some sort of genetic lineage in the roster of the "greatest" Brazilians who bequeathed important works to the history of Brazil: "care, handling, love of a Brazil that would pass, and die, legacies to a posterior Brazil, that, by being successively passed on, shall never die."[108]

In the *General Introduction* written by Rodolfo Garcia, where the author traces a brief biography of the Jesuit Fernão Cardim, the character is portrayed as "a most trustworthy informant, by admirable testimonies, which have brought plenty of light and comprehension about the phenomenon of the first colonization of country". Garcia also acknowledged Cardim as a "precursor of our History, when Brazil, so to speak, had no history yet."[109] This statement by Garcia is especially

---

107 In the case of Ferdinand Cardim *treaties*, there are also notes of Baptista Caetano, which did not receive greater attention in this study because of its central proposal to treat especially the process of annotation *Brazil General History* of Varnhagen by Capistrano Abreu and Rodolfo Garcia. Thus, the analysis of other works noted and studied the last two authors fundamentally interests us because of our main issue. GARCIA, Rodolfo. *Introducção Geral*. In: CARDIM, Fernão. *Tratados da terra e gente do Brasil*. São Paulo: Companhia Editora Nacional, 1939, p.8-9.

108 GARCIA, Rodolfo. *Introducção Geral*. In: CARDIM, Fernão. *Tratados da terra e gente do Brasil*. São Paulo: Companhia Editora Nacional, 1939,*p.9-10*.

109 GARCIA, Rodolfo. *Introducção Geral*. In: CARDIM, Fernão. *Tratados da terra e gente do Brasil*. São Paulo: Companhia Editora Nacional, 1939, *p.10-11*.

interesting due the historical epistemology that emerges from its different meanings. Was the author stating that Brazil did not have a written history, such as the *General History of Brazil,* or was he recognizing that there was no history of Brazil as there was not an independent state called Brazil by then, rather Portuguese colonies in America, given Fernão Cardim lived in the sixteenth century? His words lead us to believe that he was expressing according to the first hypothesis because history as a narrative, as written, was spelled by him in lowercase letter, for example when comparing the "history" by Gândavo to the "history" by Fernão Cardim. Meanwhile, the spelling "History" was reserved for the idea of a processual temporal phenomenon on a large scale.[110]

Fernão Cardim was therefore considered a precursor because he had not written history as expected by Rodolfo Garcia, which meant "his history is a natural rather than a civil one," he was an interesting mélange of a "geographer", an "ethnographer", "a zoologist and a botanic", although acknowledging the Jesuit also had in him "the discrete historian", being more "an eyewitness" whose reports "worth even more due to the spontaneity and the sincerity with which he candidly wrote them", than a historian who had to go through archives in order to compose his history.[111] In short, the *Treatises of the land and people of Brazil* were considered more a special source than a history book.

Thus, according to Rodolfo Garcia's discourse it became possible and necessary that Fernão Cardim was considered as one of "our first patricians", "who presided the foundation of the Brazilian nationality."[112] Considering the discursive formation in question, Cardim became not only a character in the colonial history of Brazil, especially seen from the point of view of the discourse of Brazilian nationality formation process, but also a character in the history of the establishment of the very discipline of the history of Brazil. Concomitantly it became one of the most important historical documents for the establishment of both histories, as Rodolfo Garcia argued in his *General Introduction* to the *Treatises on the land and people of Brazil.*

---

110 GARCIA, Rodolfo. *Introducção Geral.* In: CARDIM, Fernão. *Tratados da terra e gente do Brasil.* São Paulo: Companhia Editora Nacional, 1939, *p.11.*

111 GARCIA, Rodolfo. *Introducção Geral.* In: CARDIM, Fernão. *Tratados da terra e gente do Brasil.* São Paulo: Companhia Editora Nacional, 1939, *p.11.*

112 GARCIA, Rodolfo. *Introducção Geral.* In: CARDIM, Fernão. *Tratados da terra e gente do Brasil.* São Paulo: Companhia Editora Nacional, 1939, *p.11.*

However, it is also worth noting that within the critical review of Cardim's work we can observe a recurrent kind of circular "self-referencing" discursive movement as stated by Rodolfo Garcia, following the parameters that had occurred in the introductory texts to the series of documents of *First Visitation of the Holy Office*. In the *General Introduction*, the overwhelming part of the sources used to compose the narrative of Cardim's history, as well as the critical study of the *Treatises* prepared by Garcia, already are known to us through Capistrano's *Preface* to the *First Visitation* series, such as the *Annaes of the National Library*, Anchieta's writings, Varnhagen's *General History of Brazil*, without mentioning the *First visitation of the Holy officio*, quoted also in two different editions, one from 1922 and another from 1925.[113]

Again we find evidence to affirm that the critical studies of Capistrano de Abreu and Rodolfo Garcia on colonial documents were made simultaneously to the annotation of the third edition of the *General History*. Thus, we also found positive signs about the fact that such colonial documents, handled with priority by the Viscount, corroborated with his conformation as a discursive authority on the history of Brazil since the late nineteenth century to the early twentieth century. To develop and validate certain part of his *Introduction*, for example, Garcia took advantage of information extracted from a Cardim's letter dated from October 1, 1618, which, until the date of Rodolfo Garcia text composition, was unprecedented. So, until then, it was necessary to trust the Viscount's words hence the only reference to the registered letter was made by Varnhagen in his *General History*, saying it was located in the library of the Royal Academy of History of Madrid. Although acknowledging the potential doubt about the existence and contents of the letter, the word of the Viscount sufficed to Garcia. Regarding colonial documents for the writing of national history, Varnhagen seemed indeed to have the last word: "more than an advice and less than a command, an advice which one may not safely ignore."[114]

Varnhagen was the one who first brought at lights a Portuguese version of part of the Fernão Cardim's work. Until then his writings

---

113 GARCIA, Rodolfo. *Introducção Geral*. In: CARDIM, Fernão. *Tratados da terra e gente do Brasil*. São Paulo: Companhia Editora Nacional, 1939, p.12-14, 16-19.
114 ARENDT, Hannah. *Que é Autoridade?* In: *Entre o passado e o futuro*. São Paulo: Perspectiva, 2007, p.163-165.

were not even recognized as being written by him, so there were several authorships to his three treatises. In 1847, the Viscount edited a version of the *Epistolary Narrative* dedicated to the memory of Canon Januário da Cunha Barbosa, a founding member of the Historical and Geographical Institute.[115] Later, it was up to "Dr. Capistrano de Abreu" to "perform the valuable work" of presenting "clear proof" to identify the authorship of other treatises as being Fernão Cardim's. According to Rodolfo Garcia, the "services" of Capistrano to "the history of Brazil, through the listing of its sources and the interpretation of their findings were never sufficiently exalted".[116]

Another important document to be considered within the discursive institution process of Varnhagen's authority regarding "National History", through the annotation of the *General History of Brazil* done by Capistrano de Abreu and Rodolfo Garcia, is Friar Vicente do Salvador's *History of Brazil* which arises recurrently throughout the footnotes and notes of final sections in the *General History.*

In the interesting note VIII, for example, found at the end of *Section XVII - Government of D. Duarte da Costa. Attempt to Villegaignon,* of the *General History of Brazil,* Capistrano used, among other documents, Friar Vicente do Salvador's *History of Brazil* to compose an argument line opposed to Varnhagen's one about the conditions for granting the Pernambuco captaincy as an inheritance to Duarte de Albuquerque Coelho because he considered that "what is in fl. 282 v. of the book 3 of *Chancellery of Felippe I,* and that served Varnhagen's work is a copy, hence his mistake, although excusable. "An interesting fact is that Capistrano cited, as a reference for Vicente de Salvador's *History of Brazil,* the edition of 1918, which was prefaced and annotated by himself, and has counted with the collaboration of Rodolfo Garcia for proof reading the edition.[117] But the footnote number VIII did not end with comments and reviews produced by Capistrano Var-

---

115 GARCIA, Rodolfo. *Introducção Geral.* In: CARDIM, Fernão. *Tratados da terra e gente do Brasil.* São Paulo: Companhia Editora Nacional, 1939, *p.19.*

116 GARCIA, Rodolfo. *Introducção Geral.* In: CARDIM, Fernão. *Tratados da terra e gente do Brasil.* São Paulo: Companhia Editora Nacional, 1939, *p.23-25.*

117 VARNHAGEN, Francisco Adolfo de. *História geral do Brasil: antes da sua separação e independência de Portugal.* 4.ed. integral. São Paulo: Melhoramentos, 1948-1953, p.372; ABREU, J. Capistrano de. *Nota preliminar.* In: SALVADOR, Vicente do, Frei. *Historia do Brasil.* São Paulo: Melhoramentos, [1931], p.IX.

nhagen. Rodolfo Garcia also added the following passage, based on the *History* of Friar Vicente:

> Rio Branco, *Brazilian Ephemerides,* 382, Rio, 1918 assigns August 7, 1553 for the death of the donatary, who was guided by the same mistake Varnhagen has incurred. The date must be that of Jaboatão - August 7, 1554, but the place was no doubt given by Friar Vicente, according to Duarte de Albuquerque Coelho, his grandson, within the *Compendium of the Portuguese Kings,* unforeseen (copies in National Library). [. . .] - Capistrano de Abreu, *Prolegomena* to Friar Vicente do Salvador's History, ps.76. - (G.).[118]

In spite of the divergent structure of argumentation to that constructed by Varnhagen, the Viscount's discursive authority had been settled once more. What has constituted the process of the Viscount's authority is precisely the recognition operated by Capistrano de Abreu and Rodolfo Garcia when betaking a document previously used by Varnhagen to criticize him. In this case, the review must be understood as an aggregating action of meaning and credibility to the historical narrative previously prepared by Varnhagen, and not as an attack to his assumptions. The fundamentals of the Viscount's historiographical work were reinforced by the review, hence the logic construction of his historiographical narrative remained intact, that is, the privilege of using primary sources to build a narrative guided by the national point of view were not affected at all. As Hannah Arendt reminded us, "the word *auctoritas* is derived from the verb *augere,* 'to increase', and what the authority and those in possession of it constantly increase is the foundation."[119] That is why the criticism directed toward Varnhagen must be understood more as an act of rectification of the "monument" founded by the Viscount, of addition, increasing of meaning, rather than an act of denial.

In addition, once again the Viscount had primacy in handling the source. According to Capistrano, Varnhagen was possibly one of

---

118 VARNHAGEN, Francisco Adolfo de. *História geral do Brasil: antes da sua separação e independência de Portugal.* 4.ed. integral. São Paulo: Melhoramentos, 1948-1953, p.372.

119 ARENDT, Hannah. *Que é Autoridade?* In: *Entre o passado e o futuro.* São Paulo: Perspectiva, 2007, p.163-165.

the first historians - though he was "still a teenager" - to "browse the pages" of a copy of this "elusive, almost mythical book" supposedly located in the Library of the Needs, in Lisbon, which, however, was listed as vanished at the time Capistrano wrote his *Preliminary Note* to the *History* of Friar Vicente.[120]

During a special mission to the European archives, intended to find and collect important documents for writing the history of Brazil, João Francisco Lisboa discovered at the Tombo Tower one separate chapter of the work of Friar Vicente, which was later identified, printed and credited to Varnhagen in the *Journal of the Brazilian Historical and Geographical Institute*, in 1858.[121] However, so far the *History of Brazil* remained unpublished, not whole identified, even despite the fact that the Viscount has come across with the preserved codex at the Tombo Tower, which according to Capistrano was not an original one, not being even copy of the original. According to Capistrano de Abreu, on the margins of its pages there were notes "written by pencil" being quite possibly Varnhagen's autographic ones.[122]

Capistrano also said Varnhagen would have possibly used information from Friar Vicente's work to compose the second edition of the *History of the skirmish against the Dutch in Brazil* and the *General History of Brazil*, although "most of the time without identifying their origins attributing one to the words of an ancient writer, p.379, and the other, p.393, using the non-transparent initials set of F. V. of S.". Beyond keeping the manuscript confidential, Varnhagen also believed that a document entitled *Chronicle of the Custody of Brazil*, by Friar Vicente, was part of the broad collection of the *History of Brazil*.[123]

After being custodian in Bahia, Friar Vicente of Salvador returned to Portugal, and there he wrote most of his *History of Brazil*, specifically in the cities of Évora and Lisbon. Later, during the 1620s, he returned to Brazil again elected guardian of Bahia, but while he was on his way he

120 BREU, J. Capistrano de. *Nota preliminar*. In: SALVADOR, Vicente do, Frei. *Historia do Brasil*. São Paulo: Melhoramentos, [1931], *p. V-VI.*
121 ABREU, J. Capistrano de. *Nota preliminar*. In: SALVADOR, Vicente do, Frei. *Historia do Brasil*. São Paulo: Melhoramentos, [1931], p.V.
122 ABREU, J. Capistrano de. *Nota preliminar*. In: SALVADOR, Vicente do, Frei. *Historia do Brasil*. São Paulo: Melhoramentos, [1931], p. XVI-XVI I.
123 ABREU, J. Capistrano de. *Nota preliminar*. In: SALVADOR, Vicente do, Frei. *Historia do Brasil*. São Paulo: Melhoramentos, [1931], p.SAW.

was imprisoned by the Dutch, being eventually released only a few years later, finally finishing his work only on 27 December 1627.[124]

It was possibly during the period he served as custodian in a convent of the order of the "capuchos" of Santo Antônio in Bahia, that Friar Vicente do Salvador wrote the *Chronicle of the Custody of Brazil*, time in which he transited recurrently between Olinda and Bahia, between the years 1612 and 1614. Some of the pages of Friar Vicente's *History of Brazil* were possibly derived from his *Chronicle of the Custody*, as believed Capistrano de Abreu and Varnhagen. However, Capistrano insisted on the point that "to consider the *Chronicle of the Custody* as first part of this *History*, as did Varnhagen, it is to forget the size of the two, the respective composition dates, and the well-defined purpose of each."[125]

To compose the pages of the *Preliminary Note*, Capistrano drew documents we have seen appear recurrently throughout his many writings, such as Gabriel Soares, the documentary series concerning the *First Visitation of Holy Office - Confessions* and *Denunciations of Bahia*, Anchieta, Jaboatão, besides the *General History of Brazil* that in 1918, date of the *Preliminary Note,* was being annotated concurrently with the completion of the Friar Vicente's *History of Brazil* edition. The circular discursive phenomenon of self-referencing appeared again in the *Preliminary Note* Capistrano has written to the *History of Brazil*. The process adding footnotes, reviewing, and prefacing such works constitute a set of intellectual activities developed almost simultaneously to the critical annotation work of the *General History of Brazil* undertaken by Capistrano de Abreu and Rodolfo Garcia.

Finally, when beginning to conclude his *Note*, Capistrano had compared the *Chronicle of the Custody* and Vicente do Salvador's *History* to the "anonymous, not well identified yet," *Dialogues of the magnitudes of Brazil,* claiming Friar Vicente appeared "to have known then or later the author and at least part of the work because in some points, for example in the advantages of Bahia's lists, he sort of responds to it."[126]

---

124 ABREU, J. Capistrano de. *Nota preliminar*. In: SALVADOR, Vicente do, Frei. *Historia do Brasil*. São Paulo: Melhoramentos, [1931], p. XV-XVI.

125 The emphasis in italics are my responsibility. ABREU, J. Capistrano de. *Nota preliminar*. In: SALVADOR, Vicente do, Frei. *Historia do Brasil*. São Paulo: Melhoramentos, [1931], p. XIV.

126 ABREU, J. Capistrano de. *Nota preliminar*. In: SALVADOR, Vicente do, Frei. *Historia do Brasil*. São Paulo: Melhoramentos, [1931], p. XVIII.

These *Dialogues* had hitherto unknown authorship and only received a name to occupy the role of the author after an important and rigorous documentary work review done by Capistrano de Abreu. In a study first published in the *Journal of Commerce,* dated of November 24, 1900 and September 24, 1901, under the title of *Historical Journals,* but later called *Dialogues of the magnitudes of Brazil,* Capistrano credited the authorship of such writings to Ambrósio Fernandes Brandão.[127]

Regarding the importance of Friar Vicente's works, its potential to close "gaps" in Brazilian history and symbolize a history of Brazil whose actual existence would be potentially and possibly guaranteed beyond historiographical representations, Capistrano wrote about:

> The hinterland entries [sort of event similar to the *Flags* above mentioned] would have attracted attention, and the knowledge about them would not be in scout names without biographical indications and without geographical localization, like mere "subjects without predicates." Many anecdotes have been harvested, breaking the pedestrian or solemn monotony with which the Rocha Pittas, the Berredos and the Jaboatões have blasphemed publicity.
>
> Friar Vicente finished his *History of Brazil* in 1627; only a century later Sebastião da Rocha Pitta released a *History ... of the Portuguese America.*[128]

Thus, once again the discursive authority of Varnhagen was guaranteed. Through the work of critical annotation of the documents related to the colonial past of Brazil and of the *General History,* not only the bases, the foundations of his historiographical project were consolidated and perpetuated, but also the meaning implied to the narrative remained stable. The essential features were still there: a history built on a massive volume of documents critically reviewed, and a historiographical representation guided by the perspective of national history.

The last document to be scrutinized is the *Diary of Navigation by Pero Lopes de Sousa* deserves special attention. As reported by Varnhagen in his short *Prologue* to the 1867 edition of the *Diary:*

---

127 ABREU, J. Capistrano de. *Nota preliminar*. In: SALVADOR, Vicente do, Frei. *Historia do Brasil*. São Paulo: Melhoramentos, [1931], p. 297-336.

128 The emphasis in italics are my responsibility. ABREU, J. Capistrano de. *Nota preliminar*. In: SALVADOR, Vicente do, Frei. *Historia do Brasil*. São Paulo: Melhoramentos, [1931], p. X XII.

The 1st edition of Pero Lopes de Sousa's *Diary* was made in 1839, based mainly on the original codex (written by Pero Goes, with several intended and unacceptable retouches by Martim Affonso de Souza own hand), which existed in Lisbon in the Royal Library of Ajuda. This edition has been sufficiently publicized by biographers, starting with Brunet (according to Souza) and Mr. Rich in his *Bibliotheca Americana* ["*American Library*"].[129]

In this text, Varnhagen explained that he had suppressed some of the old existing footnotes, in order to give way to large reproductions of documents considered of great importance to the " National History", because the *Diary* "due to the discovery of other documents [had lost] part of the maximum value it had when it first saw the light". Varnhagen said also to have been the *Diary* one of the key documents to shed "light on several intricate issues related to the early times of our history," that enabled the critique of "Friar Gaspar's and Jaboatão's interminable conjectures."[130]

Obviously, beside the *Diary* of Pero Lopes itself, we find reproduced the following sources: some documents about Martim Affonso, "Documented Note on Fernando de Noronha Island," "Martim Affonso Donation in St. Vincent," a "complaint, in Latin, against Pero Lopes, for the destruction in 1532 of the French trading post in Pernambuco", the *Concise route of Náo Bretoá's journey,* the "Regiment given to the captain Christovam Pires", the "List of Náo Bretoá's campaign, including cabin boys and footmen", and a list about the "Load of brazil. Slaves, cats and parrots, the taking of Cabo Frio", without mentioning the "Diligence concerning the stolen tool in Bahia registered by the scrivener Duarte Fernandes ".[131]

All these documents discovered by Varnhagen in the European archives he visited were later edited and published by him. The "Book

129 VARNHAGEN, Francisco Adolfo de. *Prologo*. In: SOUSA, Pero Lopes de. *Diário da navegação de Pero Lopes de Sousa pela costa do Brazil até o Rio Uruguay (de 1530 a 1532)*. Rio de Janeiro: Typographia de D. L. dos Santos, 1867, p.3.

130 VARNHAGEN, Francisco Adolfo de. *Prologo*. In: SOUSA, Pero Lopes de. *Diário da navegação de Pero Lopes de Sousa pela costa do Brazil até o Rio Uruguay (de 1530 a 1532)*. Rio de Janeiro: Typographia de D. L. dos Santos, 1867,, P.3-5.

131 SOUSA, Pero Lopes de. *Diário da navegação de Pero Lopes de Sousa pela costa do Brazil até o Rio Uruguay (de 1530 a 1532)*. Rio de Janeiro: Typographia de D. L. dos Santos, 1867, p.113.

(on the trip) of the Náo Bretoa," for example, was "made known" by the Viscount in 1844, and "for the first time came wholly to light in 1854 at the end of the 1st volume of our General History (1st Edition, note 13, in page 427-432) - The MS. from which the copy has been taken is kept in Lisbon in the Tombo Tower (at the armoire of the House of the Crown, Sheaf 9 Num. 2)".[132]

However, in 1927, Capistrano published a new version of Pero Lopes de Sousa's *Diary of Navigation*. It was basically the same text, although this time the issue was opened by a *Preface by J. Capistrano de Abreu*. According to Abreu:

> Among the manuscripts in the Library of Ajuda Francisco Adolfo de Varnhagen discovered a volume concerning the trip of Martim Affonso de Sousa to Brazil, attributed to Pero Lopes de Sousa, his brother, donatary of the captaincies of Santo Amaro and Tamaracá. Not Barbosa Machado nor any other bibliographer had referred the work, kept in three copies, and one can imagine his shock. Comparing them he prepared a text, enriched it with precious notes and with his spare student resources he abuzz edited the *"Diary of the navigation of the fleet that went to Brazil in 1530...Lisbon, 1839 "*.[133]

Once more, Capistrano mentioned in his *Preface* documents here previously analyzed, as was the case of Friar Vicente of Salvador. However, he insisted to write down that in his edition "the historical facts appointed in the '*Diary*' have been clarified, sometimes more, sometimes less", and "some have been extracted from Castilian documents", been "brought to a Brazilian book for the first time" and "amidst the documents gathered in the second volume" some were inedited.[134] Thus, even if we could not explicitly find the movement

---

132 VARNHAGEN, Francisco Adolfo de. *Prologo*. In: SOUSA, Pero Lopes de. *Diário da navegação de Pero Lopes de Sousa pela costa do Brazil até o Rio Uruguay (de 1530 a 1532)*. Rio de Janeiro: Typographia de D. L. dos Santos, 1867, p.5.

133 *Prefacio de J. Capistrano de Abreu* to the edition of 1927 of the *Diário da navegação de Pero Lopes de Sousa* does not have page numbers. Regardless, all citations will be accompanied by references. ABREU, J. Capistrano de. *Prefacio de J. Capistrano de Abreu*. In: SOUSA, Pero Lopes de. *Diário da navegação de Pero Lopes de Sousa: 1530-1532*. Rio de Janeiro: Typographia Leuzinger, 1927, s/p.

134 ABREU, J. Capistrano de. *Prefacio de J. Capistrano de Abreu*. In: SOUSA, Pero Lopes de. *Diário da navegação de Pero Lopes de Sousa: 1530-1532*. Rio de Janeiro: Typographia Leuzinger, 1927, s/p.

of discursive self-referencing discussed before, within the *Preface by J. Capistrano de Abreu* to the 1927 edition of the *Diary*, at least we can find the recognition of Varnhagen's authority through the emulation of the belief in the fundamental value of the sources for the composition of Brazilian history and historiography, since he resorted to documents such as Friar Vicente of Salvador's writings.

Therefore, it seemed Capistrano and Garcia prudently followed Varnhagen's guidelines, by tracking, collecting, editing and criticizing essential historical sources for writing the "National History", especially those documents and narratives about the colonial past, as if these documents would give the historian a direct and efficient access to the colonial past. And this way, that process of collecting and reviewing documentation previously framed the potential reading-comprehension of them. Whilst Capistrano de Abreu and Rodolfo Garcia added footnotes to the *General History of Brazil* they also prefaced and annotated such colonial documents, discursively determining the range of possibilities for the production of statements about the history of Brazil in this kind of circular motion of self-referencing of the historic discourse. By doing it they reaffirmed Varnhagen's authority about the "National History" because he was the great handler and discoverer of documents on the colonial past, a period recognized as essential to the formation of the Nation, the State, the identity, as well as the Brazilian history. Concealed amongst footnotes and final section notes, being even referenced in Capistrano's *Preface* to the 1927 edition of the *Diary of Navigation by Pero Lopes de Sousa*, a particular work deserves special attention: the *History of Portuguese Colonization in Brazil*.[135]

---

135 ABREU, J. Capistrano.*Preface of J. Capistrano de Abreu. In:* SOUSA, Pero Lopes.*Daily navigation Pero Lopes de Sousa: 1530-1532. Rio de Janeiro: Typographia Leuzinger, 1927* s / p.

History of Portuguese Colonization in Brazil: Brazilian colonial history or the history of Portugal's colonies?

Originally published in monthly installments at the price of $5000 reis "paid on delivery", this "Monumental Commemorative Edition of the First Centenary of the Independence of Brazil" was "funded by the Portuguese Government" by ministerial order of 12 May 1919 and considered to be the case of "public interest by the national congress of the United States of Brazil" in the decree number 4643 dated from January 17, 1923.[136] However, this "high funding" barely exceeded the limits of a demonstration of support to the publication of the *History of Portuguese Colonization in Brazil*. Among the contemporary sources that were used to compose the footnotes added to Varnhagen's *General History of Brazil* by Capistrano de Abreu and Rodolfo Garcia, we can safely consider that the *History of Colonization* is one of the most recurrent, playing an important role in the conformation of Varnhagen's discursive authority regarding the possibilities of making certain sets of statements about the "National History".

This chapter will focus on how some kind of circular discursive process of self-referencing was built between the two histories in question. I shall describe a quite similar process to the case discussed in the previous chapter, regarding the work of collecting, reviewing, and publishing colonial historical sources by Capistrano de Abreu and Rodolfo Garcia. The role this process played on the discursive conformation of Varnhagen as the major authority on the history of Brazil, especially considering the colonial past will be discussed aiming the theoretical and epistemological implications of this phenomenon. In addition, we will also address, although briefly, the history of the writing and production of the *History of Portuguese Colonization in Brazil*.

---

136 The information taken from the *History of Portuguese Colonization of Brazil* that do not have numbered pages were taken from *the National lithograph Tribute by* Carlos Malheiros Dias and Albino de Sousa Cruz, in whose pages there is no numbering. *Tribute to National Lithography.in:* DIAS, Carlos Malheiro (Org.). *História da colonização portuguesa do Brasil. Edição monumental comemorativa do primeiro centenário da Independência do Brasil.* Porto: Litografia Nacional/ Sociedade Editora da Historia da Colonização Portuguesa do Brasil, 1921-1924, s/p... .

Writing the *History of Portuguese Colonization in Brazil*

The *History of Portuguese Colonization in Brazil*, this "Monumental Commemorative Edition of the First Centenary of the Independence of Brazil", was organized and sponsored by Portuguese colonies resident in Brazil, especially the colonies of Rio de Janeiro and Pará, as part of the numerous commemorative efforts of the early twentieth century, among which were included, for example, the commemorations of Vasco da Gama's expedition (1898), the IV Centenary of the Discovery of Brazil (1900), or the Centenary of the Opening of the Ports (1908).[137]

> Fernando Catroga noted that the commemoration of the centenary of the Independence of Brazil in Portugal was characterized by a reduced historiographical expression and this shyness was customary in the celebrations of the Portuguese State. The publishing of the *HPCB [History of Portuguese Colonization in Brazil]*, in this sense, was an exception, but it was a private venture, sponsored by the elite of the Portuguese colony in order to strengthen the Portuguese-Brazilian "approximation". The participation of the Portuguese State was limited to the recognition of its "utility" and the tax exemption on the purchase of paper. [138]

---

137 ALVES, Jorge Luís dos Santos. *Malheiro Dias e o luso-brasileirismo: um estudo de caso das relações culturais Brasil-Portugal.* Tese de Doutorado. Orientadora: Profa. Dra. Lúcia Maria Bastos Pereira das Neves. Rio de Janeiro: Universidade do Estado do Rio de Janeiro/Programa de Pós-graduação em História, 2009, p.258-264; Of celebrations and commemorative nature of events at the beginning of the twentieth century Brazil, see: GUIMARÃES, Lúcia M. Paschoal. *Circulação de saberes, sociabilidades e linhagens historiográficas: dois congressos de História Nacional (1914 e 1949).* In: GUIMARÃES, Manoel Luiz Salgado (Org.). *Estudos sobre a escrita da história.* Rio de Janeiro: 7Letras, 2006, p.162-181; _____. IV Congresso de História Nacional: tendências e perspectivas da história do Brasil colonial (Rio de Janeiro, 1949). *Revista Brasileira de História*, São Paulo, v.24, n.48, p.145-170, 2004..Text available http://www.historia.uff.br/tempo/artigos_livres/artg18-7.pdf. Accessed 29/09/2010.

138 "Only in 1923, however, the Publishing Society of History of the Portuguese colonization of Brazil obtained the exemption from import duties of paper for printing and the abolition of export duties of Portuguese books.(...) According

In 1918, José Augusto de Magalhães, president of the Chamber of Commerce and Industry of Para, suggested that a great commemorative work was carried out in order to ensure the defense of the Portuguese heritage in Brazil. At the time, there were a lot of harsh controversies on the pages of magazines, books, and weeklies about the character of the formation of Brazilian nationality, especially regarding whether it had more affinity or opposition to the Portuguese nationality. Thus, the function of the Portuguese element in the formation of the Brazilian State and Nation, as well as the possible institutional relations between Portugal and Brazil, received special attention in the public debate among learned men involved in these issues.[139]

to the editors, the collection would have a circulation of 25,000 copies expected *folio*, distributed booklets to subscribers. However, sales would have been set at 20,000 copies. Of this amount, 14,000 copies have been sold in Brazil and the other in Portugal. The selling system in fascicles was designed by Sousa Cruz to reduce costs so that the edition would finance itself. This option was not original and suited to the restricted publishing both in Brazil and Portugal, although printing costs in the latter were lower. The preference for printing in Europe was motivated by economic factors (high manufacturing costs and depreciation of the Brazilian currency) and the best technical and aesthetic quality. According Hallewell, in the late nineteenth century, "typographic works in Rio became two times more expensive than in Europe: graphic illustration services could cost three times more." In fact, the collection was printed in Portugal, at the National Lithographic Company between 1921 and 1926 ".ALVES, Jorge Luís dos Santos. *Malheiro Dias e o luso-brasileirismo: um estudo de caso das relações culturais Brasil-Portugal*. Tese de Doutorado. Orientadora: Profa. Dra. Lúcia Maria Bastos Pereira das Neves. Rio de Janeiro: Universidade do Estado do Rio de Janeiro/Programa de Pós-graduação em História, 2009, p.270-271, 280.

139 "The awareness of Brazil for the celebrations had strong symbolic motivation present in other later similar celebrations: Brazil was the empirical rebuttal of criticism that sought to deny the civilizing mission of Portuguese colonialism." ALVES, Jorge Luís dos Santos. *Malheiro Dias e o luso-brasileirismo: um estudo de caso das relações culturais Brasil-Portugal*. Tese de Doutorado. Orientadora: Profa. Dra. Lúcia Maria Bastos Pereira das Neves. Rio de Janeiro: Universidade do Estado do Rio de Janeiro/Programa de Pós-graduação em História, 2009, p.270-271, 280. About the literary polemics and on the issue of public discussions about the possible nature of the formation of national identity occurred more generally from the 1870s until the early twentieth century, Roberto Ventura wrote that "due to the proximity of opponents the discussions formed a *reflective and dual standard* of debate, which can be related to horizontal forms and poorly differentiated social and political conflict at the time. Although polemicists seek to emphasize that opposition predominated because of the relative lack of theoretical

Considering these relations, which the author Jorge Luis Alves dos Santos called the "*lusobrasileirismo*" [Portuguese-Brazilian], we can consider that on one hand there were the so called *lusófilos*, advocates of the Portuguese heritage and culture regarding the Brazilian national formation, and not reticent to the presence and the function of Portuguese immigrants residing in the country; on the other hand, the "*lusófobos*", those people resistant to Portuguese influence and discordant of the idea of a positive Portuguese heritage for Brazil. To the "*lusófobos*", among which the author considered especially the roles of Manoel Bomfim, Álvaro Bomílcar, Antônio Torres, and João Ribeiro, Brazil had become a country full of vices and flaws, precisely because of its colonial past and the civilizational model the Portuguese had applied to the country, which was considered equally full of vices and faults. In short, the Portuguese colonization process applied to Brazil was characterized as highly exploratory, being a kind of persistent "curse", whose consequences the country still suffered in the course of those first decades of the twentieth century.[140]

In this sense, within such debates about the role of Portugal and the Portuguese regarding Brazil, the *History of Colonization* emerged during this period as a project of huge importance, trying to increase the appreciation of the Portuguese immigrant and of the past arising from the Portuguese colonization action in Brazil. However, these were not the sole issues involving the production context of the referred work. In the first decades of the twentieth century there were at stake in Portugal as well as in Brazil, issues concerning the formation of the State and the Nation, when the Portuguese First Republic (1910-1926) had recently been instituted.[141]

---

and ideological differences until the first decades of the twentieth century. The similarities were generally more relevant than the alleged differences between the opponents, who threw themselves to personal attacks as a way to rhetorically emphasize their individuality and originality. VENTURA, Roberto. *Estilo tropical: história cultural e polêmicas literárias no Brasil, 1870-1914*. São Paulo: Companhia das Letras, 1991, p.78-80.

140 ALVES, Jorge Luís dos Santos. *Malheiro Dias e o luso-brasileirismo: um estudo de caso das relações culturais Brasil-Portugal*. Tese de Doutorado. Orientadora: Profa. Dra. Lúcia Maria Bastos Pereira das Neves. Rio de Janeiro: Universidade do Estado do Rio de Janeiro/Programa de Pós-graduação em História, 2009, p.146-154.

141 "Thus, the various texts that composed to, especially those written by Malheiro

For the publishing project of the *History of Portuguese Coloniza-tion in Brazil* to be achieved the group gathered around José Augusto de Magalhães, constituted of the most prominent members of the elite of Portuguese immigrant colonies in Brazil, considered to be of great importance to found an institution that controlled the edito-rial process of the *History of Colonization*. Thus they founded the Pu-blishing Society of the History of Portuguese Colonization of Brazil, located on the symbolic street Luís de Camões, number 30, in Rio de Janeiro, whose duties were divided as it follows: "a board composed by Carlos Malheiro Dias (literary direction), Albino Souza Cruz (finan-cial management), Roque Gameiro (artistic director) and counselor Ernesto de Vasconcellos (cartographic direction)".[142]

However, the task of producing and organizing the *History of Colonization* was under the responsibility of certain specific fellows, namely: Albino Sousa Cruz and Carlos Malheiro Dias, two of the most important names of the Portuguese colony in the city of Rio de Janeiro.

Founder of Souza Cruz & Cia, a company linked to processing and marketing of tobacco and its derivatives, Albino Sousa Cruz, in 1919, negotiated the procedures for the editing process and raised most of the necessary capital for the realization of *History of Portu-guese Colonization in Brazil*, also participating in the articulation "for the visit of the President of Portugal, António José de Almeida, to the Centennial celebrations". Sousa Cruz became very influential not only in the Portuguese colony in Rio de Janeiro, as well as in the broader context of Portuguese-Brazilian relations. Albino came to be

---

Dias, echoed the political and ideological conflicts that divided the Portuguese society, especially the elites, in the first third of the twentieth century. "ALVES, Jorge Luís dos Santos. *Malheiro Dias e o luso-brasileirismo: um estudo de caso das relações culturais Brasil-Portugal.* Tese de Doutorado. Orientadora: Profa. Dra. Lúcia Maria Bastos Pereira das Neves. Rio de Janeiro: Universidade do Estado do Rio de Janeiro/Programa de Pós-graduação em História, 2009, , p.275.

142 ALVES, Jorge Luís dos Santos. *Malheiro Dias e o luso-brasileirismo: um estudo de caso das relações culturais Brasil-Portugal.* Tese de Doutorado. Orientadora: Profa. Dra. Lúcia Maria Bastos Pereira das Neves. Rio de Janeiro: Universidade do Esta-do do Rio de Janeiro/Programa de Pós-graduação em História, 2009, p.146-154. *Homenagem da Litografia Nacional.* In: DIAS, Carlos Malheiro (Org.). *História da colonização portuguesa do Brasil. Edição monumental comemorativa do primeiro centenário da Independência do Brasil.* Porto: Litografia Nacional/ Sociedade Edi-tora da Historia da Colonização Portuguesa do Brasil, 1921-1924, s/p..

acclaimed by his peers and admirers as a "patron of the Portuguese
-Brazilian history."[143]

Carlos Malheiro Dias, on the other hand, can be considered
the main intellectual articulator for the production of the *History of
Colonization*. Journalist, novelist, and historian, member of the Royal
Portuguese Reading Cabinet, of the Brazilian Academy of Letters
(curious and symbolically occupying the chair hold before by Eça
de Queiróz, one of the most important Portuguese writers from the
nineteenth century), the Portuguese Academy of History, and the
Academy of Sciences of Lisbon. Malheiro Dias acquire a degree in
Literature, at the University of Lisbon in 1899, institution where had
also graduated names like Cesário Verde and Eugênio de Castro, "two
of the main Portuguese poets from the second half of the nineteenth
century", as well as the Brazilian historian Oliveira Lima, which was
the only Brazilian name to collaborate with the production of the
History of Portuguese Colonization in Brazil.[144]

---

143 "Albino Sousa Cruz (1874-1966) migrated to Brazil in 1885.In Rio de Janei-
ro, he was employed in the cigarette factory of José Francisco Correia (Earl of
Agrolongo) and worked there for 18 years. In 1903, he founded the Souza Cruz
& Cia. (Company Souza Cruz) and in 1914 joined the British capital. Practical-
ly withdrawn from business, Sousa Cruz devoted himself to philanthropy and
community life of the Luso-Brazilian associations. He was president of the Royal
Portuguese Reading Cabinet (1919-1962) and president of the Federation of
Portuguese Associations in Brazil (1941). From the 30's, after the death of José
Júlio Pereira de Moraes (Moraes viscount), Sousa Cruz became the main leader-
ship of the Portuguese community in Rio de Janeiro and Brazil. "ALVES, Jorge
Luís dos Santos. *Malheiro Dias e o luso-brasileirismo: um estudo de caso das relações
culturais Brasil-Portugal.* Tese de Doutorado. Orientadora: Profa. Dra. Lúcia Ma-
ria Bastos Pereira das Neves. Rio de Janeiro: Universidade do Estado do Rio de
Janeiro/Programa de Pós-graduação em História, 2009, p.275.
144 "Carlos Malheiro Dias was born in Porto on 13 August 1875. The father, Henrique Malheiro Dias, was representative of a French insurance company and the
mother, Adelaide Carolina Araújo Pereira was natural of Brazil's Rio Grande do
Sul. The Brazilian descent through his mother has always been emphasized by
Malheiro Dias, mainly in moments of stirring up the controversy that was involved with Brazilian antagonists. The family origins of the mother's side, in this
sense, acted as individual and emotional identity strengthening the historical and
cultural ties between Brazil and Portugal. Paternal grandparents, on the other
hand, were from the parish of Santa Eulalia de Barrosa, traders entered in the
liberal bourgeoisie and awarded honorary favors the consolidated regime in the
years 1820/1830. " ALVES, Jorge Luís dos Santos. *Malheiro Dias e o luso-brasilei-*

In addition, Malheiro Dias received considerable public recognition during the decades of 1910-30. Some of his books, such as trilogy composed of *Son of the herbs, The Teles d'Albergaria* and *Passion of Mary Heaven,* written between the years 1900 and 1902, gave him recognition both in Brazil and Portugal, making Malheiro Dias a prominent author in the Portuguese-Brazilian writing scenario. Other works, however, as was the case of *The mulatta,* eventually bequeathed him the fame of being "anti-Brazilian". The fictional narrative in question was considered an "insult to the nationality [Brazilian], a demonstration of the pernicious character of the Portuguese", a "wordy and moralizing" repository of bigoted and misogynistic ideas.[145]

Carlos Malheiro Dias was also a writer and chronicler of everyday facts of Lisbon and Rio de Janeiro, having written for the magazine *O Cruzeiro* and *Revista da Semana.* He became partner of Arthur Brandão and Aureliano Machado at the American Publisher Company, owner of the *Revista da Semana.* The weekly *O Cruzeiro,* was founded by Dias in 1928, granting him considerable fortune and financial security, as well as greater popularity not only among members of the Portuguese colonies in Brazil, but also amidst Brazilian readers. Moreover, Malheiro Dias achieved considerable success in his literary career, fact that supplied him of great non-literary opportunities, such as his nomination to the post of ambassador at the Portuguese embassy in Spain close to the end of his life. Initially sympathetic to Salazar, Malheiro Dias gradually observed the authoritarian excesses of Salazar's dictatorship, subsequently averting from the regime.[146]

---

rismo: um estudo de caso das relações culturais Brasil-Portugal. Tese de Doutorado. Orientadora: Profa. Dra. Lúcia Maria Bastos Pereira das Neves. Rio de Janeiro: Universidade do Estado do Rio de Janeiro/Programa de Pós-graduação em História, 2009 p.186-187, 190-193.

145 ALVES, Jorge Luís dos Santos. *Malheiro Dias e o luso-brasileirismo: um estudo de caso das relações culturais Brasil-Portugal.* Tese de Doutorado. Orientadora: Profa. Dra. Lúcia Maria Bastos Pereira das Neves. Rio de Janeiro: Universidade do Estado do Rio de Janeiro/Programa de Pós-graduação em História, 2009, p.211-219, 241-243.

146 ALVES, Jorge Luís dos Santos. *Malheiro Dias e o luso-brasileirismo: um estudo de caso das relações culturais Brasil-Portugal.* Tese de Doutorado. Orientadora: Profa. Dra. Lúcia Maria Bastos Pereira das Neves. Rio de Janeiro: Universidade do Estado do Rio de Janeiro/Programa de Pós-graduação em História, 2009, p.199-205-208.

The botched nomination for ambassador to Spain in February 1935, would be the reward for his adherence to the regime or, in the words of Sarmento Pimentel, Salazar "haltered him with the promise of making him ambassador of Madrid." Perhaps the embassy was something more transcendental than a reward or a cunning action by Salazar. For Augusto de Castro, it was a teenage aspiration and the official acclamation of Malheiro Dias' moral and material existence.

The uncertainty about the effectiveness of the embassy, due to the severity of several subsequent health problems (jaundice followed by stroke) that simultaneously struck Malheiro Dias brought him disappointments, when he was already passing through financial and family issues.[147]

Regarding his historiographical works, in addition to his important role in the publishing of the *History of Portuguese Colonization in Brazil,* his "proximity to the elite of the colony" assured him, in 1895, the opportunity to "get two 'contos de réis' [an erstwhile Brazilian currency] from António Gomes Avelar (Earl of Avelar) for writing a history of the Portuguese Beneficence."[148] Moreover, he was a correspondent member of the Capistrano de Abreu Society, a historical literary club founded in September 11, 1927, at Capistrano's former home in Rio de Janeiro.[149]

---

147 ALVES, Jorge Luís dos Santos. *Malheiro Dias e o luso-brasileirismo: um estudo de caso das relações culturais Brasil-Portugal.* Tese de Doutorado. Orientadora: Profa. Dra. Lúcia Maria Bastos Pereira das Neves. Rio de Janeiro: Universidade do Estado do Rio de Janeiro/Programa de Pós-graduação em História, 2009, p.208.

148 ALVES, Jorge Luís dos Santos. *Malheiro Dias e o luso-brasileirismo: um estudo de caso das relações culturais Brasil-Portugal.* Tese de Doutorado. Orientadora: Profa. Dra. Lúcia Maria Bastos Pereira das Neves. Rio de Janeiro: Universidade do Estado do Rio de Janeiro/Programa de Pós-graduação em História, 2009, p.191.

149 A list of the names of members of Capistrano Abreu Society can be found at the end of every book published by the Company, such as the end of *Ensaios e Estudos.* ABREU, J. Capistrano de. *Ensaios e estudos: (crítica e história).* 1. série. Rio de Janeiro: Sociedade Capistrano de Abreu, 1931, p.351-359 "On September 11, 1927, it was created in the city of Rio de Janeiro The Capistrano de Abreu Society, an institution with the deliberate order to 'preserve' the memory of the late historian Capistrano de Abreu. The Company continued its activities for 42 years and gathered significant representatives of national and foreign literary field, as Mário de Andrade, Manuel Bonfim, Assis Chateaubriand, Cascudo, Franz Boas, Paul Rivet and HG Wells. In these four decades, the institution has owned the most significant leaders and whose actions were more forceful

Thus, at the end of the collection (Volume III began to be published in 1924), it [the *History of Portuguese Colonization in Brazil*] was presented by the printers to the National Lithographic Company as the resulting confluence of intelligence and work. First, Malheiro Dias, the intellectual capital: "Because scientifically and literary, this masterpiece is almost exclusively possible due to his tracing and outlining. He was the architect and the worker of this prodigious construction". Later, but not in a less important level, Sousa Cruz represented the financial capital and practical sense required for the achievement of the project. [...] Both the intellectual and the capitalist were highlighted due to their patriotism, abnegation spirit, and initiative, which along with the "copious resources given by the Portuguese colony of Brazil" enabled the *HPCB*. [150]

However, it is important to also evaluate who were the other authors responsible for the composition and writing of the *History of Portuguese Colonization in Brazil*. Portuguese distinguished literati of the 1920s formed this group almost absolutely, the only exception being the presence of the Brazilian diplomat and historian Manuel de Olivei-

---

in building Capistrano's memory, historians Paulo Prado, Rodolfo Garcia and Jose Honorio Rodrigues. "SILVA, Itala Byanca M. da. Annotating and prefacing the work of the "master": reflections of Jose Honorio Rodrigues on Capistrano de Abreu. *History of Historiography*. n.3, p.83-105, September / 2009, p.84.Text available at: http://www.ichs.ufop.br/rhh/index.php/revista/article/viewFile/55/35. Accessed on 04/01/2011; "Abreu Capistrano Company had an organization similar to the IHGB. The guild consisted of intellectuals divided into membership levels, i.e. effective partner (110 jobs), corresponding member or honorary (30 jobs).However, the number of partners is a demonstration of the unique and distinctive character of this institution in relation to its contemporaries. The IHGB, for example, had its amount of active members limited by the number 50. However, the conveyor character of Capistrano de Abreu Society, at least in its first incarnation, was not defined only by an intellectual affinity, but by a practice based on the exercise of friendship and 'cult' to Capistrano de Abreu, so the number as high membership. "SILVA, Ítala Byanca M. da. Os discípulos de Capistrano de Abreu: Paulo Prado e o "Caminho do Mar". *Anais, Programa e Resumos da XXVI Reunião Anual da Sociedade Brasileira de Pesquisa Histórica*. Rio de Janeiro: 2006. Text available at: http://sbph.org/reuniao/26/trabalhos/Jorge%20Luis%20Santos%20Alves.pdf .Accessed 18/05/2010.

150 ALVES, Jorge Luís dos Santos. *Malheiro Dias e o luso-brasileirismo: um estudo de caso das relações culturais Brasil-Portugal*. Tese de Doutorado. Orientadora: Profa. Dra. Lúcia Maria Bastos Pereira das Neves. Rio de Janeiro: Universidade do Estado do Rio de Janeiro/Programa de Pós-graduação em História, 2009, p.278.

ra Lima, who was responsible for writing the history on the captaincy of Pernambuco. Besides his degree in the *"Curso Superior de Letras"* [Literature] in Lisbon, he inaugurated the chair of Brazilian studies at the Faculty of Arts at the University of Lisbon in 1923. Oliveira Lima was also member of the Brazilian Historical and Geographical Institute and professor at the Catholic University in Washington.[151]

Initially designed to compose five volumes, the *History of Colonization* ended consisting of only three volumes, named respectively and ordinarily as *The precursors of Cabral, The epic of the coastline*, and *The Brazilian Middle Age (1521-1580)*.

> The first part of *HPCB* (volumes I and II) favored the background of Cabral's journey; the evaluation of the state of nautical art, cartography, and astronomy in Portugal during the fifteenth century; the first contacts with the native people and the geographic recognition of the coast. The second part (Volume III) deals with the effective beginning of the land occupation and conquest by the installation of Hereditary Captaincies (the captaincy of Pernambuco, New Lusitania, was the only one to have a unique chapter) and the General Government (Governments of Tomé de Sousa and Duarte da Costa).[152]

According to Malheiro Dias, the number of Brazilian authors would increase at the volumes IV and V, to be published from the second half of the 1920s, which were never published though. Among the Brazilian authors that should have been in such a project, the name Afrânio Peixoto particularly stands out. Peixoto was president of the Brazilian Academy of Letters during this period and coordinated along with other Brazilian intellectuals, among them Capistrano and

---

151 ALVES, Jorge Luís dos Santos. *Malheiro Dias e o luso-brasileirismo: um estudo de caso das relações culturais Brasil-Portugal.* Tese de Doutorado. Orientadora: Profa. Dra. Lúcia Maria Bastos Pereira das Neves. Rio de Janeiro: Universidade do Estado do Rio de Janeiro/Programa de Pós-graduação em História, 2009,; about the work of Oliveira Lima in IHGB, and the situation of the institution at the time, see: GUIMARÃES, Lúcia M. Paschoal. *Da escola palatina ao silogeu: Instituto Histórico e Geográfico Brasileiro (1889-1938).* Rio de Janeiro: Museu da República, 2007.
152 ALVES, Jorge Luís dos Santos. *Malheiro Dias e o luso-brasileirismo: um estudo de caso das relações culturais Brasil-Portugal.* Tese de Doutorado. Orientadora: Profa. Dra. Lúcia Maria Bastos Pereira das Neves. Rio de Janeiro: Universidade do Estado do Rio de Janeiro/Programa de Pós-graduação em História, 2009, p.286-287.

Garcia as mentioned above, a huge effort to publish two great collections of rare works that addressed the "national classics" of Brazilian literature and history.[153] Such final volumes were intended to cover the gap ranging from the second half of the sixteenth century unto the Second Empire age in the nineteenth century. According to Alves, it would have transformed the *History of Portuguese Colonization in Brazil* into a history of Brazil.[154]

Besides Carlos Malheiro Dias, stood out among the various Portuguese authors the following names: Antônio Baião, Jaime Cortesão, Júlio Dantas, and Carolina Michäelis de Vasconcelos.

Graduated by the law school of the University of Coimbra, Antônio Baião was an important Portuguese historian and archivist. Baião worked for many years at the National Archives of the Tombo Tower and was member of the Lisbon Academy of Sciences and the Portuguese Academy of History. As reported by Capistrano de Abreu and Rodolfo Garcia, the credits of the discovery in the Tombo Tower as well as the publication in the journal of the institution of the series of documents related to the *First Visitation of the Holy Office* are largely due to Antônio Baião. Moreover, the chapters *The trade of Pau Brazil* within the second volume and the *Expedition of Cristóvão Jacques* within the third volume were under Baião's editorial assignment. [155]

Besides being a doctor, Jaime Cortesão was also an important historian, writer, and politician. Jaime Cortesão worked for many ye-

153 GARCIA, Rodolfo. *Introducção Geral*. In: CARDIM, Fernão. *Tratados da terra e gente do Brasil*. São Paulo: Companhia Editora Nacional, 1939, *p.7*.

154 ALVES, Jorge Luís dos Santos. *Malheiro Dias e o luso-brasileirismo: um estudo de caso das relações culturais Brasil-Portugal*. Tese de Doutorado. Orientadora: Profa. Dra. Lúcia Maria Bastos Pereira das Neves. Rio de Janeiro: Universidade do Estado do Rio de Janeiro/Programa de Pós-graduação em História, 2009, p.284.

155 ABREU, J. C.. *Introdução*. In: MENDOÇA, Heitor Furtado de. *Primeira visitação do Santo Officio ás partes do Brasil pelo licenciado Heitor Furtado de Mendoça: Denunciações da Bahia (1591-1593)*. São Paulo: Ed. Paulo Prado, 1925, p.7; GARCIA, Rodolfo. *Introducção*. In: MENDOÇA, Heitor Furtado de. *Primeira visitação do Santo Officio ás partes do Brasil pelo licenciado Heitor Furtado de Mendoça: Denunciações de Pernambuco (1593-1595)*. São Paulo: Ed. Paulo Prado, 1929, p.XXXIII; ALVES, Jorge Luís dos Santos. *Malheiro Dias e o luso-brasileirismo: um estudo de caso das relações culturais Brasil-Portugal*. Tese de Doutorado. Orientadora: Profa. Dra. Lúcia Maria Bastos Pereira das Neves. Rio de Janeiro: Universidade do Estado do Rio de Janeiro/Programa de Pós-graduação em História, 2009, p.289-290, 292.

ars at the National Library of Portugal, but due to the Portuguese political crisis at the beginning of the century and the escalation of conflicts of World War II, he moved to Rio de Janeiro where he taught and devoted himself to research on the history of Portuguese navigations of the sixteenth century, being Cortesão the responsible for writing the chapter *The expedition of Cabral* within the second volume.[156]

Júlio Dantas also graduated in medicine and was a reputed writer of theater plays and journalist. Dantas was president of the Academy of Sciences of Lisbon for forty years and under his pen was assigned the writing of the chapter *The Manuelina Age* for the first volume. The philologist Carolina Michäelis de Vasconcelos, a professor at the University of Lisbon was in charge of the transcription, reproduction, and commentaries on the famous letter by Pero Vaz de Caminha, which recorded the supposed first Portuguese contact with American lands. The letter is reproduced in the second volume of the *History of Portuguese Colonization in Brazil.*[157]

Finally, considering the chapters assigned to Carlos Malheiro Dias, on whose life and career we discussed earlier, we can say that he was responsible for the largest set of texts present in the *History of Colonization,* composing such texts a total of 8 chapters. First, he was responsible for writing the introduction of the first and third volumes. Regarding the second volume, Malheiro Dias was responsible for chapters *The Vera Cruz Week, The Expedition of 1501*, and *The Expedition of 1503*. For the third volume he composed *The Expedition of Cristovão Jacques, The metropolis and its achievements during the reigns of Dom João III, Dom Sebastião, and Cardinal Dom Henrique*, and *The feudal regime of the captaincies.*

An important feature of this set of texts is that the narratives are guided by a storyline in which the heroic aspect of the Portuguese

156 ALVES, Jorge Luís dos Santos. *Malheiro Dias e o luso-brasileirismo: um estudo de caso das relações culturais Brasil-Portugal.* Tese de Doutorado. Orientadora: Profa. Dra. Lúcia Maria Bastos Pereira das Neves. Rio de Janeiro: Universidade do Estado do Rio de Janeiro/Programa de Pós-graduação em História, 2009, p.290-291.

157 ALVES, Jorge Luís dos Santos. *Malheiro Dias e o luso-brasileirismo: um estudo de caso das relações culturais Brasil-Portugal.* Tese de Doutorado. Orientadora: Profa. Dra. Lúcia Maria Bastos Pereira das Neves. Rio de Janeiro: Universidade do Estado do Rio de Janeiro/Programa de Pós-graduação em História, 2009, p.282-283, 290-292.

colonization is highlighted, as well as the heritage of Portuguese traditions that would partly generate the Brazilian people.[158] The Portuguese colonization of America was thus shaped as historiographical narrative in the *History of Colonization* to ensure the colonizing process established in Brazil as the greatest example of fostering Portuguese culture and traditions in distant lands. Moreover, according to Alves, "this image stretched the Portuguese Golden Age to the contemporary and justified new imperial pretensions, this time, in order to form a third empire in Africa, where the *'lusíadas'* after the rediscovery of the greatness of the past would create 'new Brazils'.[159]

---

158 About how the narrative structure of the historiographical discourse relates to the critical selection of the things that will make it possible to be built, as well as about the status of historiographical narrative and the epistemological implications of this reflection, the literary critic Hayden White proposed in his controversial and discussed book called *Metahistory,* the historiographical narrative necessarily has a fictional character despite its characteristics and potential scientific pretensions. According to White, which argues according to the topological theory of discourse, the very discursive field determines the language is above all a mediation between reality and cognition of a subject. And this discursive field is formed by a conceptual field that prefigures and mediates our understanding of reality as well as our experience. Finally, Hayden White argues that occur prefigured plots of historiographical narratives according to the way, and mediated by discursive and conceptual field, the historian orders and has the facts within the framework of his narrative. In *Metahistory,* White proposed a typological combination of "entanglements" *(employment)* and epistemological structuring foundations of narrative and the possibility of historiographical knowledge from the analysis of the works of important historians and philosophers of history of the nineteenth century, such as Burckhardt, Michelet, Ranke and Tocqueville among the first, and Hegel, Marx, Nietzsche, and Croce among the last. WHITE, Hayden. *Metahistory: the historical imagination in nineteenth-century Europe.* Baltimore/London: The Johns Hopkins University Press, 1975; _____. *Trópicos do discurso: ensaios sobre a crítica da cultura.* São Paulo: Edusp, 2001.

159 The *"lusíadas"* is a reference to *The Lusíadas,* an epic poem from the sixteenth century by the very acknowledged Portuguese poet Luís de Camões, constituting a story of the Portuguese discoveries and navigations of the referred period. ALVES, Jorge Luís dos Santos. *Malheiro Dias e o luso-brasileirismo: um estudo de caso das relações culturais Brasil-Portugal.* Tese de Doutorado. Orientadora: Profa. Dra. Lúcia Maria Bastos Pereira das Neves. Rio de Janeiro: Universidade do Estado do Rio de Janeiro/Programa de Pós-graduação em História, 2009, p.265; _____. *A memória do lusobrasileirismo na historiografia brasileira: a "História da Colonização Portuguesa do Brasil.* In: Anais, Programa e Resumos da XXVI Reunião Anual da Sociedade Brasileira de Pesquisa Histórica. Rio de Janeiro: 2006. http://sbph.org/reuniao/26/trabalhos/Jorge%20Luis%20Santos%20Alves.pdf.

In that context, it bulged within the first decades of the twentieth century a focused literature for the aggrandizement of this special relationship with the valorization of Portuguese colonization as the root of Brazilian society. Thus, the edition of *History of Portuguese Colonization in Brazil* (hereinafter abbreviated as *HPCB)* stood out as an emblematic work of the discourse for the Portuguese-Brazilian approach, had been thought as a contribution of the Portuguese colony to the independence centenary celebrations in 1922.

On the one hand, the *HPCB* was part of a particular political and cultural context, marked by the emphasis on the discourse about the nation and nationality, and on the other, it was going to meet a particular aspect of this context that was the inclusion of a certain memory of the Portuguese-Brazilianism (imaginary, perceptions, and sensitivities) in Brazilian history, the preservation of which was linked to the interests of economic and intellectual elites of the Portuguese colony.[160]

In short, the history of the Portuguese colonies in America structured along the pages of the *History of Portuguese Colonization in Brazil* managed this historical narrative in order to represent the history of Brazilian colonial period until the national independence as a long process of continuity in which the Portuguese heritage had central importance. Thus, the Brazil from the early twentieth century, specifically that of the first two decades, seemed to represent to the authors of that work all the credit and glory of both the Portuguese settlers of the colonial past and those from the republican present, as well as of those Brazilians who perpetuated or could still perpetuate such a civilizational project.

---

160 ALVES, Jorge Luís dos Santos. *Malheiro Dias e o luso-brasileirismo: um estudo de caso das relações culturais Brasil-Portugal.* Tese de Doutorado. Orientadora: Profa. Dra. Lúcia Maria Bastos Pereira das Neves. Rio de Janeiro: Universidade do Estado do Rio de Janeiro/Programa de Pós-graduação em História, 2009, p.267.

"The actual national point of view":
The "National History" between two monuments

After a brief presentation on the history of the *History of Portuguese Colonization in Brazil,* we should delve a little more on said work analysis to get closer to the central question posed in this study, i.e., to question about how the footnotes added to the *General History of Brazil* by Capistrano de Abreu and Rodolfo Garcia collaborated to establish the discursive authority of Francisco Adolfo Varnhagen regarding Brazilian history, from the second half of the nineteenth century until about the first half of the twentieth century when it was finally published the fourth critical edition annotated by Rodolfo Garcia in 1953. Concerning this critical annotation process of the *General History of Brazil,* the *History of Portuguese Colonization in Brazil* performed an important and interesting role, especially considering the space historiographical works contemporary to Capistrano and Garcia occupied in the notes. Along with documents recently published or reproduced in the notes – especially in those at the final sections of chapters –, as well as the several monographs, and editions of the *Journal of the Brazilian Historical and Geographical Institute* (BHGI), the great recurrence of references to the *History of Portuguese Colonization in Brazil* draws us attention. Thus, we will observe more acutely the conformation process of the discourse on national history around Varnhagen's name and work during that period.

The existing proximities between the *General History* and the Portuguese "Monumental Edition" of Brazilian history were much higher than the aspirations to official aspect and limited official support they received from their government institutions or experts. The *History of Colonization,* as previously stated, stamped on numerous pages of its monthly installments, the acknowledgment of the "high funding of the Portuguese Government" and the Decree number 4643 of January 17, 1923, according to which the work was considered of "public interest by the national congress of the United States of Brazil."[161]

---

161 *Homenagem da Litografia Nacional.* In: DIAS, Carlos Malheiro (Org.). *História da colonização portuguesa do Brasil. Edição monumental comemorativa do primeiro centenário da Independência do Brasil.* Porto: Litografia Nacional/ Sociedade Edi-

The *General History of Brazil,* on the other hand, had its first two editions published during its author lifetime, and had limited royal and BHGI institutional support, although the protection granted by the Institute is debatable and restricted. The "high funding of the Portuguese Government" to the *History of Portuguese Colonization* was more symbolic than functional, not exceeding the costs of the paper to print the work. In the *General History* case the BHGI support must be understood more due to the function that Varnhagen held in one of the committees dedicated to discover important documents to the history of Brazil in European archives, to the opportunities the Viscount got to publish texts and documents discovered by him in the *Journal* of the BHGI, as well as the symbolic support of being awarded by the Institute for one of his texts, since the *General History* did not get the official stamp of the Institute.[162]

Besides sharing the epithet of "monuments", they also shared a theoretical conception of history, the criteria of selection of sources, and the national perspective, which guided their historical narratives. It can be argued that there was a sort of identification relationship and mutual endorsement of discourses. Let us begin by the reasoning of the arguments.

In the *History of Portuguese Colonization in Brazil* "the force of arguments is based upon an indestructible foundation of documentation". As stated within the text of introduction to the work, "the work referenced all sources for the study of Brazilian history", "making detailed reference to any literature concerning the versed theme."[163] It means

---

tora da Historia da Colonização Portuguesa do Brasil, 1921-1924, s/p..

162 GUIMARÃES, Lúcia M. Paschoal. Debaixo da Imediata Proteção de Sua Majestade Imperial. O Instituto Histórico e Geográfico Brasileiro (1838-1889). *Revista do Instituto Histórico e Geográfico Brasileiro*. Rio de Janeiro, a.156, v.1, n.388, p.459-613, jul./set., 1995, p.498-501, 558-561; According to Lúcia Guimarães, Varnhagen's image in the IHGB would have been rehabilitated over the first two initial decades of the twentieth century, mainly due to the discovery of the manuscripts of the *History of the Independence of Brazil* in the Baron of Rio Branco files in Itamaraty Palace. (...)*Da escola palatina ao silogeu: Instituto Histórico e Geográfico Brasileiro (1889-1938)*. Rio de Janeiro: Museu da República, 2007, p.89-90, 115-125.

163 DIAS, Carlos Malheiro. *Introdução*. In: DIAS, Carlos Malheiro (Org.). *História da colonização portuguesa do Brasil. Edição monumental comemorativa do primeiro centenário da Independência do Brasil.* Porto: Litografia Nacional/ Sociedade Editora da Historia da Colonização Portuguesa do Brasil, 1921-1924, p.XXXV.

that regarding the subject of Portuguese colonization in Brazil as stated by the title, a common theme also to the *General History of Brazil,* the Portuguese book offered a whole set of sources and references.

An important part of the primary documents used in the *History of Colonization* coincides with the sources used by Varnhagen while writing his *General History,* which were subsequently validated by his annotators as previously argued, such as Friar Vicente of Salvador, Gândavo, Friar Gaspar de Madre Deus, Fernão Cardim, the *Seraphic Orb* by Friar Antônio de Santa Maria Jaboatão, and the *Diary* of Pero Lopes de Sousa, edited by Varnhagen in 1839. Many of these documents were discovered, critically evaluated, revised, and/or edited by the Viscount and his annotators. The very *Introduction* of the *History of Colonization* begins with an epigraph of the *General itinerary* by Gabriel Soares de Souza, which was originally discovered and edited by Varnhagen.[164]

Furthermore, there were quotations from and references to several volumes of the *Journal of the Historical and Geographical Brazilian Institute,* of journals of some Brazilian regional Historical Institutes, as well as works by Capistrano de Abreu and Varnhagen. The organizers of the *History of Portuguese Colonization in Brazil* widely used information taken from the first, second, and even third editions of the *General History of Brazil* to compose their work. A curious fact, hence this work is one of the most used by Capistrano, and especially by Rodolfo Garcia, during the process of adding footnotes to the *General History* during the period ranging from 1907 to 1927. Whilst

---

164 DIAS, Carlos Malheiro. *Introdução.* In: DIAS, Carlos Malheiro (Org.). *História da colonização portuguesa do Brasil. Edição monumental comemorativa do primeiro centenário da Independência do Brasil.* Porto: Litografia Nacional/ Sociedade Editora da Historia da Colonização Portuguesa do Brasil, 1921-1924, p.XXXV. "Varnhagen discovered and / or edited several basic documents for the history of Brazil, for example , and just about material XVI century, a unheard of Friar Luis de Sousa, clarifying the expedition of Christopher Jacques; the *Daily navigation,* Pero Lopes de Sousa; documents on diplomatic problems between Francis I and John III; the book Nau Bertoa, 1511; *Narrative Letter Writing* Fernão Cardim; and the *Treaty* of Gabriel Soares de Sousa, whose authorship defined and the text established definitively in the edition of 1851." Wehling Arno. *State, history, memory: Varnhagen and the construction of national identity. Rio* de Janeiro: New Frontier, 1999, p.140; CEZAR, Themistocles. When a manuscript becomes historical source: the true marks on account of Gabriel Soares de Souza (1587). *História em revista.* Pelotas, v. 6 (dez. 2000), p. 37-58.

the *History of Portuguese Colonization in Brazil* is used as source for the critical annotation of Varnhagen's *History* by Capistrano and Garcia, the Viscount's masterpiece is used as document at the *History of Portuguese Colonization*. Both "monumental" works used each other as secondary sources. The authors of the *History of Portuguese Colonization in Brazil* used the Viscount's "monument" as a way to consolidate their own historiographical discourse, while Capistrano and Garcia used the *History of Portuguese Colonization of Brazil* as an important contemporary work to support the critical annotation project of the *General History*. I believe that within this circle of discursive self-referencing the monumental aspect so exalted in Varnhagen's *History* was also desired and sought by the organizers and authors of the Portuguese edition. Analyzing some excerpts from the *History of Portuguese Colonization,* especially the *Introduction* written by Carlos Malheiro Dias, we can see this occurring as follows below:

> Monument erected with high and patriotic intents, the *History of Portuguese Colonization in Brazil* was considered worthy to serve as a model for a similar project designed by the Madrid Geographical Society and the Royal Spanish Academy of History.
>
> Due to the authority of its contributors, the importance of the documents it embodied, the critical amendments it makes on the many events it analyzes, this work is considered the greatest monument so far written to elucidate and reliably interpret the history of Brazil. [165]

The multiple laudatory passages present in the Introductions by Malheiros Dias led us to believe the organizers and authors of the *History of Portuguese Colonization in Brazil* considered they had built "the greatest monument so far written to elucidate and reliably interpret the history of Brazil" in order to "represent [not only] the contribution of the Portuguese in Brazil to celebrate the centennial of Independence of the largest Latin nation on earth, born from the womb of Portugal", as well as symbolizing the importance of the contribution made by the numerous Portuguese settlers during the colonial period

---

165 DIAS, Carlos Malheiro. *Introdução*. In: DIAS, Carlos Malheiro (Org.). *História da colonização portuguesa do Brasil. Edição monumental comemorativa do primeiro centenário da Independência do Brasil.* Porto: Litografia Nacional/ Sociedade Editora da Historia da Colonização Portuguesa do Brasil, 1921-1924, p.XXXV.

in the history of the country, indicating a direction to the national history of Brazil according to which the Portuguese people would have essential function.[166] Although this is an introductory text full of laudatory rhetoric, it seems that the Portuguese organizers aspired rather inserting Portugal within Brazilian history than the opposite, namely, inserting Brazil in Portuguese national history.

This sense implied to the narrative of colonial history would mean that the history of Brazil was conformed since the Portuguese navigations of the sixteenth century, and through the subsequent evolution from the condition of colony to the condition of "largest Latin [independent] nation on earth", emanating a glory halo toward the ancient metropolis that at the time of production of the History of Colonization Portuguese in Brazil, went on through a series of traumatic political events. Thus, the History of Portuguese Colonization should "be in the future the most beautiful and the purest glory of this sad period of national Portuguese abasement".167 Certainly the first

---

166 On the implication of meaning to an event or set of events through their linguistic expression and discourse structure, and the self-reference phenomenon of speech, Paul Ricoeur said that "if all speech is updated as an event, all discourse is understood as meaning ".According to the author, when we communicate an experience is precisely the sense that imply the construction of its linguistic expression, i.e. its constitution in a speech, not the events and experiences that we had with them. RICOEUR, Paul. *Teoría de la interpretación. Discurso y excedente de sentido*. Cidade do México: Siglo XXI Editores, 2006, p.24-26; *Homenagem da Litografia Nacional* In: DIAS, Carlos Malheiro (Org.). *História da colonização portuguesa do Brasil. Edição monumental comemorativa do primeiro centenário da Independência do Brasil*. Porto: Litografia Nacional/ Sociedade Editora da Historia da Colonização Portuguesa do Brasil, 1921-1924, s/p..

167 *Homenagem da Litografia Nacional* In: DIAS, Carlos Malheiro (Org.). *História da colonização portuguesa do Brasil. Edição monumental comemorativa do primeiro centenário da Independência do Brasil*. Porto: Litografia Nacional/ Sociedade Editora da Historia da Colonização Portuguesa do Brasil, 1921-1924, s/p.;; On the relationship between the political moment experienced by the Portuguese in the early twentieth century with the establishment of the First Republic and its relation to the production of the *History of Portuguese Colonization of Brazil*, Jorge Alves said that "on the one hand, there was the discussion of the position of Portugal and Portuguese in Brazil, in which the *HCP* was part of a recovery project of the Portuguese presence and on the other, the *HCP* was linked to the national question in Portugal during the period of the First Republic (1910-1926).Thus, the various texts that composed it, especially those written by Malheiro Dias, echoed the political and ideological conflicts that divided the Portuguese society,

two decades of the twentieth century were a crucial moment in the history of Portugal.

> In Brazil, the abolition of slavery in 1888 was a key event, sealing the fate of the monarchy, already profoundly opposed due to its "excessive centralism", in the means that it withdrew its ultimate support: that of the last enslavers of the country. In this sense, the Republic has been established through a coup-d'état but it had been a long way coming and found no major resistances. In Portugal, the Republic was preceded by traumatic events such as the murder of Dom Carlos and the heir Prince Luís Felipe, in 1908.[168]

Therefore, the authors of the *History of Portuguese Colonization* seemed to try to retrieve some of Portugal's former glory during this "sad period of national abasement" - in which the Portuguese monarchy had ended, replaced by a still vacillating republic - by conducting a grand narrative about the history of the Portuguese colonization in Brazil. It seems they wanted to absorb some of the glory of its former colony, which had not only become independent a century ago, but was also a seemingly promising republic. It was like the prodigal son was praised in order to extol the achievements of the mother, to glorify "the contribution of the Portuguese in Brazil to celebrate the centennial of Independence of the largest Latin nation on earth, born from the womb of Portugal". Or maybe it was an attempt to show that despite such a "sad period of national abasement" Portugal still had its past glory, mainly seen through the eyes of its former colony.

Regarding the prefiguration of the past in history, more specifically in national history, we can see that the former Portuguese colonies in America prefigured in their narratives the future Brazilian national State in both Varnhagen's *General History of Brazil* and in the *History of Portuguese Colonization in Brazil*. On the writings by

---

especially the elites, in the first third of the twentieth century. "ALVES, Jorge Luís dos Santos. *Malheiro Dias e o luso-brasileirismo: um estudo de caso das relações culturais Brasil-Portugal*. Tese de Doutorado. Orientadora: Profa. Dra. Lúcia Maria Bastos Pereira das Neves. Rio de Janeiro: Universidade do Estado do Rio de Janeiro/Programa de Pós-graduação em História, 2009, p.275.

168 GOMES, Ângela de Castro. *A República, a história e o IHGB*. Belo Horizonte: Argvmentvm, 2009, p.95-96.

Friar Gaspar de Madre Deus, which were widely used by Varnhagen in his *General History*, Capistrano and Garcia stated that "he is the most complete representative of the patriot and parochial chronicler", adding that may be necessary "to make the Benedictine friar one of the most representative figures of the Brazilian colonial society".[169] However, even more interesting was the fact they considered the first century of existence of the Portuguese colonies in America as precisely the period of "*The Brazilian Middle Age (1521-1580)*".[170]

During the first decades of the twentieth century, especially until the 1940s, it has been developed amidst some of the most reputed members of the Brazilian lettered elite, such as Capistrano de Abreu and Sílvio Romero among others, an intense debate of political and cultural ideas, in which historiography occupied a prominent place. Its main question was to determine the causes of the "delay" in the development of the country and the essential characteristics of the formation of the "Brazilian nation", so that it would be possible to formulate a civilizational project of "modernization" for Brazil. Moreover, hence Brazil had ceased to be an empire and become a republic such intellectuals considered the challenge to modernize the country would be a necessary step forward the national development. It seemed natural to those learned men that the future would be certainly better after the monarchical regime and the enslaver society.[171]

> The Centenary [of the Independence] mobilized the Brazilian elites in order to celebrate the National-State foundation. If the recognition of the state as a historical and political reality was unani-

---

169 DIAS, Carlos Malheiro. *Introdução*. In: DIAS, Carlos Malheiro (Org.). *História da colonização portuguesa do Brasil. Edição monumental comemorativa do primeiro centenário da Independência do Brasil*. Porto: Litografia Nacional/ Sociedade Editora da Historia da Colonização Portuguesa do Brasil, 1921-1924, p.XXXVIII.

170 *Homenagem da Litografia Nacional* In: DIAS, Carlos Malheiro (Org.). *História da colonização portuguesa do Brasil. Edição monumental comemorativa do primeiro centenário da Independência do Brasil.* Porto: Litografia Nacional/ Sociedade Editora da Historia da Colonização Portuguesa do Brasil, 1921-1924, s/p..

171 GOMES, Ângela de Castro. *A República, a história e o IHGB*. Belo Horizonte: Argvmentvm, 2009, p.21-29; VENTURA, Roberto. *Estilo tropical: história cultural e polêmicas literárias no Brasil, 1870-1914*. São Paulo: Companhia das Letras, 1991; ver também: SEVCENKO, Nicolau. *Literatura como missão: tensões sociais e criação cultural na Primeira República*. São Paulo: Companhia das Letras, 2003.

mous, the same, however, could not be said about the second half, namely, the nation. The nationality remained a vast field of digressions and philosophic, literary, and political speculations, which fed the political culture, the political myths, and literature. Thus, at the beginning of the 1920s, expressions of nationalist groups and the modernist movement in literature and arts signaled the national question as a central focus of the intellectual and political life.[172]

However, not only in Brazil but also in Portugal it strengthened a concept of history notably characterized by notions such as progress and national history, able to sustain a liberal national state formation project. Such "liberal state project" postulated in both countries a proposal for a republic that would necessarily conduct the development of such states and nations. In Portugal, the progress would be conditioned to its full integration to the other contemporary European powers. In Brazil, it was about modernizing and inserting the country in the "concert of civilized nations."[173]

Rodolfo Garcia presented a proposal of bibliographical classification for Brazilian libraries along the pages of his *Systems of Bibliographic Classification: On the decimal classification and its advantages*, "monograph presented to the consideration of the Historical Institute on October 20, 1914" containing a brief history on such classification systems and on modern systems of bibliographic production.[174] The interesting fact is that Rodolfo Garcia established a curiously congruent characterization of the colonial period of the sixteenth century to that one featured on the *History of Portuguese Colonization in Brazil* as the "*Brazilian Middle Age (1521-1580)*". These discursive statements have presented a conception of modern history that can be characterized as progressive, teleological, temporally ordered in linear way, and directed according to a specific end which makes time acqui-

---

172 ALVES, Jorge Luís dos Santos. *Malheiro Dias e o luso-brasileirismo: um estudo de caso das relações culturais Brasil-Portugal*. Tese de Doutorado. Orientadora: Profa. Dra. Lúcia Maria Bastos Pereira das Neves. Rio de Janeiro: Universidade do Estado do Rio de Janeiro/Programa de Pós-graduação em História, 2009, p. 268.

173 GOMES, Ângela de Castro. *A República, a história e o IHGB*. Belo Horizonte: Argvmentvm, 2009, p.96.

174 GARCIA, Rodolfo. *Sistemas de classificação bibliográfica: da classificação decimal e suas vantagens*. Rio de Janeiro: Associação Brasileira de Bibliotecários, 1969, p.11, 13-19.

res qualitative characteristics.

According to the author, this was a time that could be classified as *"Primitive period (1500-1530)"* followed by *"Colonization (1530-1624)"*.[175] In other words, the sixteenth century, notorious for being characterized as colonial period, was recognized not only by the authors of the *History of Portuguese Colonization in Brazil* as well as by Rodolfo Garcia as an initial period and, in a way, as a negative period in the history of Brazil. "Initial period" because both works stated that the sixteenth century was the beginning of the development of what would become Brazil and its history. "In a negative way", because on one hand, this period was characterized as the "Brazilian Middle Age," and the concept "Middle Ages" has been widespread disseminated since the eighteenth century on, becoming a "fixed historical periodization *topos*" in the nineteenth century often loaded with pejorative sense. On the other hand, it is described as "primitive", i.e. not evolved because, as stated above and in accordance with the concept of modern history, the historical timeline implies qualitative characteristics.[176]

In order to leave the "primitive" stage of development, Brazil should enter into another historical path, namely the "Colonization". Therefore, the Portuguese colonization of America in the past would have removed Brazil - or rather, removed that early stage of communal feeling the authors conformed as the future national state since the colonial past - from a "primitive" stage that was not even colonial, to a subsequently positive stage. Within this structure consisting of stages that follow or precede each other, the colonial period was taken as an important formative stage of the modern Brazilian state. It would have been specifically through the period called "Colonization" that the future nation would have left its primitive condition. This historiographical form of ordering and classifying suggests a "qualitative demand" of the historical time as it makes it seems natural that every subsequent time must necessarily be new or even better than the previous periods because it represents a greater repository of experience.[177]

---

175 GARCIA, Rodolfo. *Sistemas de classificação bibliográfica: da classificação decimal e suas vantagens*. Rio de Janeiro: Associação Brasileira de Bibliotecários, 1969, p.36.
176 KOSELLECK, Reinhart. *Futuro Passado, Contribuição à semântica dos tempos históricos*. Rio de Janeiro: Contraponto/Ed.PUCRJ, 2006, p.271; _____. *historia/Historia*. Madri: Editorial Trotta, 2004, p.17.
177 KOSELLECK, Reinhart. *Futuro Passado, Contribuição à semântica dos tempos*

However, there is a fundamental difference between the two classifications. It would be hard to imagine that the Portuguese authors characterized the sixteenth century of the colonial history of Brazil in a specifically negative way. That was the very golden age of Portuguese history. It is from the end of the fifteenth century and more especially during the sixteenth century that the Portuguese kingdom met his splendor through the Discoveries and the great transoceanic navigations, not only expanding the glory of Portugal, as well as its wealth, influence, and power within the European national context as also in several locations such as Africa, Asia and America. Even despite the ongoing process of historiographical criticism about the golden age of Portuguese history during the mid-nineteenth century - such as the desecration of the Battle of Ourique by Alexandre Herculano, a Portuguese historian and writer - it was still possible to find, within the pages of the *History of Portuguese Colonization in Brazil,* a considerable exaltation of the Battle of Alcácer Kibir.[178]

---

históricos. Rio de Janeiro: Contraponto/Ed.PUCRJ, 2006, p.274.

178 A critical discussion quite interesting about Portuguese history and its golden periods, as well as on their respective mythical interpretations, is in the *solemnia amount* of Alexandre Herculano, set of texts which can be considered as possibly being next to the *Critical Reflections* of Varnhagen, one of the first records of theoretical reflections on history written in Portuguese. According to Jose Honorio Rodrigues, "the *Reflections* of Varnhagen of *reviews,* the first critical application, *solemnia Verba* Alexandre Herculano, the first expression of rigorous unknown European critical methods of Brazilian historiography, are completed with the wonderful introduction of Capistrano de Abreu to Friar Vicente do Salvador's *History Brazil,* published in 1918. These are three essential moments of the methodology and Brazilian historiography. "RODRIGUES, José Honório. Varnhagen: o primeiro mestre da historiografia brasileira (1816-1878). *Revista de Historia de America,* Mexico n.88 (jul./dic. 1979), p.101-102; HERCULANO, Aexandre. *Solemnia verba: cartas ao senhor A. L. Magessi Tavares sobre a questão actual entre a verdade e uma parte do clero.* Lisboa: Imprensa Nacional, 1850"In that context, the nineteenth-century Portuguese historiography turned to the extirpation of metahistorical explanations of the past of Portugal as was the case of the desecration of the Battle of Ourique by Alexandre Herculano. Historical. Research that has focused on the one hand, on the collection and publication of documentary *corpus* and on the other, in the exaltation of the origins of the nation-state, the maritime expansion and the Portuguese overseas empire. "ALVES, Jorge Luís dos Santos. *Malheiro Dias e o luso-brasileirismo: um estudo de caso das relações culturais Brasil-Portugal.* Tese de Doutorado. Orientadora: Profa. Dra. Lúcia Maria Bastos Pereira das Neves. Rio de Janeiro: Universidade do Estado

The claim that the colonial period represented the "Brazilian Middle Age" gives way to certain semantic possibilities. First, classifying the colonial past of Brazil as "Middle Age" inserts the existence of the Brazilian national state and its history into a greater temporal and phenomenal structure of human history, and provides a sense of identity and temporal continuity of this object along said temporal structure. Second, it gives an idea of progressive time. Also there is the possibility of understanding that, if Portugal was entering Modernity with its great deeds and achievements, a stage that came after the period of the European Middle Ages, the future of its colony could follow the same path. However, this discourse claims a distance in the historical development of the colony in relation to that of the metropolis. Thus, according to the classification discussed above, it is implied in the title of the third volume, "The Brazilian Middle Age" that only Portugal had entered the "new era" of Modernity during the sixteenth century.

Therefore, despite the potentially negative feature that the concept of "Middle Age" could imply, the positive discourse of the Portuguese colonization of Brazil could be strengthened not only in relation to the Portuguese point of view, but also in relation to the Brazilian point of view, according to the claim that during the heyday of Portugal 's modern history would have been laid the foundations for the development of the future Brazilian national state, which during its "Colonization" was in its "Dark Ages." The first day of March, 1565, for example, was considered by Malheiro Dias as "a memorable date in the fasti of the Brazilian Middle Ages. Estácio de Sá disembarked with his soldiers at the foot of the "Pão de Açúcar" and laid the foundation of the first city of S. Sebastião do Rio de Janeiro, so named in memory of the young knight king."[179]

do Rio de Janeiro/Programa de Pós-graduação em História, 2009, p.288; DIAS, Carlos Malheiro. *Introdução*. In: DIAS, Carlos Malheiro (Org.). *História da colonização portuguesa do Brasil. Edição monumental comemorativa do primeiro centenário da Independência do Brasil*. Porto: Litografia Nacional/ Sociedade Editora da Historia da Colonização Portuguesa do Brasil, 1921-1924, p.LXII.

179 DIAS, Carlos Malheiro. *Introdução*. In: DIAS, Carlos Malheiro (Org.). *História da colonização portuguesa do Brasil. Edição monumental comemorativa do primeiro centenário da Independência do Brasil*. Porto: Litografia Nacional/ Sociedade Editora da Historia da Colonização Portuguesa do Brasil, 1921-1924, p.LX; "In this sense, as a development of Portuguese nationality in America, Brazilians suf-

The Portuguese State could even be going through a "sad period of national abasement", however, there was a time when Portugal lead the world nations development. However, it is important to look more closely at the writings of some authors of the *History of Portuguese Colonization in Brazil* so we can understand how the discourse on the history of Brazil constituted along the pages of said work, collaborated to conform Varnhagen's discursive authority, especially considering its important role in the footnotes written by Rodolfo Garcia and Capistrano de Abreu.

First, we will cover the pages written by Carlos Malheiro Dias, especially his introductions. As argued earlier, during the first decades of the twentieth century there was a recurrent concern among Brazilian intellectuals and a few Portuguese writers about the historical process of Brazilian national formation, as well as on the then currently Brazilian socioeconomic development process. Among Brazilians, we can highlight the important role of authors such as Capistrano de Abreu, Sílvio Romero, José Veríssimo, Manuel Bomfim, Euclides da Cunha, Oliveira Lima, and Oliveira Vianna among many others. From the Portuguese side it is important to highlight Jaime Cortesão who taught in Rio de Janeiro, and Carlos Malheiro Dias who were lead authors for doing such a reflection among diverse means, such as novels, poems, journals, historical studies and especially in the *History of Portuguese Colonization in Brazil*. Thus, the reference to names like Sílvio Romero and Capistrano de Abreu within the pages written by Malheiro Dias is in a certain way quite expected.

History of Brazil taught by the biography of its offspring and *The Portuguese Element* written by Silvio Romero, are recurrently referenced.[180] Romero elaborated a set of important texts in which he outlined his theory on the formation of Brazilian nationality, espe-

---

fered from a centuries-old heritage and thus components of a lineage rooted in a tradition dating back to the medieval past of Europe. "ALVES, Jorge Luís dos Santos. *Malheiro Dias e o luso-brasileirismo: um estudo de caso das relações culturais Brasil-Portugal*. Tese de Doutorado. Orientadora: Profa. Dra. Lúcia Maria Bastos Pereira das Neves. Rio de Janeiro: Universidade do Estado do Rio de Janeiro/ Programa de Pós-graduação em História, 2009, p.286.

180 DIAS, Carlos Malheiro. *Introdução*. In: DIAS, Carlos Malheiro (Org.). *História da colonização portuguesa do Brasil. Edição monumental comemorativa do primeiro centenário da Independência do Brasil*. Porto: Litografia Nacional/ Sociedade Editora da Historia da Colonização Portuguesa do Brasil, 1921-1924, p.V, X, XIV, XV, LXII.

cially within the perspective of racialist sociological theories that credited the results and conditioning of Brazilian people evolution to miscegenation as well as to some environmental influence.[181]

However, although there appears to be a considerable distance between the historiographical speeches between Varnhagen, author of a historiography style focused on the narrative of great facts and men of history, and Romero, more marked by the sociological thought and appreciation of miscegenation, some important congruence should be discussed. As it was for the Viscount, the XVI century has received special attention in Romero's studies. For Romero, this period could be characterized as "the most interesting of our history" because it would represent "history in its most intimate face", during which there was "the creation and development of those institutions that relate to the economic, artistic and domestic life of a nation."[182] In short, resurfaced the discourse according to which the colonial period, especially the sixteenth century, was considered as the foundation, as the basis of formation of the future Brazilian national state. Also according to Romero, a major problem for the Brazilian historiography was the lack of documents required for the writing of national history, especially documents that would enable the creation of a more "internal" and "cultural" narrative of Brazilian history.

> It is within this perspective that he considers that "the strongest workers of our inner progress" were the Jesuit priests, among which he highlights Anchieta. The life of this Jesuit would have this "more appreciated public face" but would have another - more private and intimate - that "deserves more interest to the social history of our country", being a mirror "to show the state of the country during the first century of the conquest and colonization."[183]

181 See:VENTURA, Roberto. *Estilo tropical: história cultural e polêmicas literárias no Brasil, 1870-1914*. São Paulo: Companhia das Letras, 1991; e TURIN, Rodrigo. *Narrar o passado, projetar o futuro: Sílvio Romero e a experiência historiográfica oitocentista*. Dissertação de Mestrado. Orientador: Prof. Dr. Temístocles Cezar. Porto Alegre: UFRGS, IFCH - Departamento de História, Programa de Pós-Graduação em História, 2005.

182 ROMERO *apud* GOMES, Ângela de Castro. *A República, a história e o IHGB*. Belo Horizonte: Argvmentvm, 2009, p.114.

183 ROMERO *apud* GOMES, Ângela de Castro. *A República, a história e o IHGB*. Belo Horizonte: Argvmentvm, 2009, p.114.

Therefore, despite the theoretical differences between Varnhagen's and Romero's historiographies, two elements remained fundamental to the writing of "National History", namely the use of primary documents of the colonial past and the guiding perspective under the national point of view, criteria that was rectified by Capistrano de Abreu and Rodolfo Garcia for the annotation of the *General History of Brazil*, and also found in the pages of the *History of Portuguese Colonization in Brazil*.

In the *introduction* to the third volume of the *History of Portuguese Colonization in Brazil*, Carlos Malheur Dias recurrently references a certain group of colonial documents, which have been previously found in the footnotes and end of section written by Capistrano and Garcia for the *General History of Brazil*. *The History of Brazil* by Friar Vicente do Salvador appears numerous times, as well as the *History of the Province of Santa Cruz* by Gândavo, and Gabriel Soares de Souza who wrote *On the wonders of Bahia* and *General Itinerary*.[184] Similarly to the notes of the *General History of Brazil*, beyond such documents as the *Annals of the National Library* and multiple numbers of the *Historical and Geographical Institute* academic journal were still used with considerable frequency. As stated earlier, these documents were mostly discovered, collected, criticized and/or edited by Varnhagen, Capistrano and/or Garcia. Capistrano himself received privileged space in Malheiro Dias's text. *"Brief traces of the history of Brazil"* and" *Brazil its natural resources and its industries"*, and the third edition of the *General History of Brazil*, have been referenced within Dias' text.[185] It is noteworthy that *General History of Brazil* appeared not only in the annotated edition by Capistrano and Garcia, but also in its second edition.[186]

184 DIAS, Carlos Malheiro. *Introdução*. In: DIAS, Carlos Malheiro (Org.). *História da colonização portuguesa do Brasil. Edição monumental comemorativa do primeiro centenário da Independência do Brasil*. Porto: Litografia Nacional/ Sociedade Editora da Historia da Colonização Portuguesa do Brasil, 1921-1924, p.I, V, X, LV-LVI, LVIII, LXI.

185 DIAS, Carlos Malheiro. *Introdução*. In: DIAS, Carlos Malheiro (Org.). *História da colonização portuguesa do Brasil. Edição monumental comemorativa do primeiro centenário da Independência do Brasil*. Porto: Litografia Nacional/ Sociedade Editora da Historia da Colonização Portuguesa do Brasil, 1921-1924,p. V, VI, IX-X, LXII.

186 Referencing the *prologue* of the second edition of the *General History of Brazil*, Malheiro Dias added that "Varnhagen, who had no Portuguese descent, recog-

Within the fifth chapter of the second volume, titled *"Cabral's Expedition" (1500)*, written by the Portuguese historian Jaime Cortesão, we find an interesting discussion in which Varnhagen's authority on "National History" was affirmed in a thought-provoking way. The discussion was centered on the document that originated the image representation of Pedro Alvares Cabral reproduced in *"pictures and praise of Men and Women"*. *However, before appearing in the text, is in the footnote number (55) that the following information is found:*

(55) The picture, through which Pedro Alvares Cabral is vulgarly presented, is reproduced within the *"pictures and praise of Men and Women"* (Lisbon, 1817). Its editors do not mention the source of that image. It is possible, however, that they had copied it from some antique painting or picture, because they did that with other of the portrayed. Be that as it may, the picture we just sketched, outlined in the documents, consists singularly with the features that represent him within the *"Men and Women"*. *Another supposed iconographic document is the bust of the Jeronimos' medallion*, which happens to represent Pedro Alvares. The four medallions well deserved a serious study representing busts of navigators, upon the pillars of one of the rows of carved Jeronimos. Varnhagen, the more rigorous of the authors to refer to the case, says in his *"historical and descriptive News of the Monastery of the Jeronimos"* (Lisbon, 1842): "In the five large frontal pillars at the gates of the confessional booths are seen also in horizontal line the sun and then four busts in medallions, which it is believed to represent the East with the four Portuguese heroes who had gone there when there came the construction; that is, it seems, Gama and his brother, Nicolau Coelho and Cabral. The latter bust confirms the tradition, because it has the face turned to the side opposite to the Sun, thus celebrating his lucky discovery of the Western Lands or Brazil. "Teixeira d'Aragão in *"Vasco da Gama and the Vidigueira"*, *referring to the first three, comes to the point of classifying them as the most authentic portraits of the heroes they represent. Until today the guards of the cloister repeat, guar-*

nizes that among the other nations of the continent, Brazil 'was that the one that cost more effort and more jobs to its settlers."DIAS, Carlos Malheiro. *Introdução*. In: DIAS, Carlos Malheiro (Org.). *História da colonização portuguesa do Brasil. Edição monumental comemorativa do primeiro centenário da Independência do Brasil*. Porto: Litografia Nacional/ Sociedade Editora da Historia da Colonização Portuguesa do Brasil, 1921-1924, p. XIII.

ding the tradition. And from them we learnt that every year the director of the Casa Pia, attached to the monastery, orders, on the occasion of the celebration of the day of the discovery of Brazil, to cover in flowers and palms the alleged bust of Cabral. That the busts represent navigators is not to be doubted. To authenticate them, their heads were dressed with the sea glengarry of that time. And as far as allows the graceful styling carved by the chisel, it is possible to affirm that the first of the busts resembles the better known of the portraits of Gama. For Varnhagen very likely happens what the tradition says. It is worth pondering, however, that Fr. Jacinto St. Miguel, when writing in the early eighteenth century *(Monastery of Belem,* manuscript published by Martinho da Fonseca) does not make any reference to this tradition.[187]

First, Varnhagen was characterized as "the most rigorous of the authors that refers to the case" and therefore as possibly one of the most reliable ones, because on that case the minutia was related to the care with the search and review of primary documents about the history of Brazil. Second, what consolidated Varnhagen's speech was his juxtaposition to tradition. By stating that "For Varnhagen very likely happened what tradition says", Cortesão established a relationship of continuity and identity with this historic speech, which not only reinforced the discourse of Varnhagen - which, according to Cortesão, was amended and strengthened by tradition - but his own. Even though the Portuguese historian stated "that Fr. Jacinto St. Miguel, when writing in the early eighteenth century *(Monastery of Belem,* manuscript published by Martinho da Fonseca) does not make any reference to this tradition", that is, with the possibility of dissonance between of Varnhagen's discourse and said Fr. Jacinto St. Michael's, Varnhagen's thesis had, for Cortesão, a greatest authoritative potential than the other different authors, because it was endorsed by tradition and by his expertise on criticism of sources.

In *General History of Brazil* we find similar statements by Varnhagen about the weight of tradition. According to the Viscount is

187 CORTESÃO, Jaime. *A expedição de Cabral (1500)*. In: DIAS, Carlos Malheiro (Org.). *História da colonização portuguesa do Brasil. Edição monumental comemorativa do primeiro centenário da Independência do Brasil.* Porto: Litografia Nacional/ Sociedade Editora da Historia da Colonização Portuguesa do Brasil, 1921-1924, p.21.

the "tradition, in harmony with some documents, [what] makes us believe."[188] But we also find, curious speeches and evidence related to Capistrano and Garcia's practices regarding the eminently positive value of tradition. In the footnote number (30), not only Capistrano placed himself in line of continuity and identity with Varnhagen through the emulation of a particular act of the Viscount, as well as Rodolfo Garcia placed himself in Capistrano's line by referring to him as "eminent master, first annotator of this book. "Continuity line in which Garcia became heir of the annotation task of his "eminent master." [189] The capital letters in parentheses indicate the authors, being (A.) to Varnhagen (Author) and (G) for Rodolfo Garcia.

> (30) *"The Caramuru before History"*, dissertation written by the author of this *history*, awarded by the Hist. Institute. Of Rio de Janeiro, in the *Publication,* 10, 129. The same author gave the prize (a gold medal) for the same Institute to offer it in future competitions. - (A.). - In 1917, the History Institute established again awards to remarkable works on history, Geography and Ethnography, and one of these (gold medals) was given, with absolute justice, to "The *language of Cashinahua"*, written by the eminent master and first annotator of this book, Capistrano Abreu, who, making use of the 'precedent opened by well deserving Francisco Adolfo de Varnhagen, Glory of the Homeland and luster of this house,' he offered to the Institute the same prize for another contest. - Conf. *Rev. of Inst. History, 82* (1917), the.790-791. - (G.). [190]

---

188 VARNHAGEN, Francisco Adolfo de. *História geral do Brasil: antes da sua separação e independência de Portugal.* 4.ed. integral. São Paulo: Melhoramentos, 1948-1953, p.307.

189 In his inaugural speech to the chair to which he was elected at the Brazilian Academy of Letters, Rodolfo Garcia made sure to outline the line to the Brazilian historiography in which he was inserted, i.e. Varnhagen, Capistrano de Abreu, and later the author himself. Interestingly, Garcia had inherited the chair created specifically for Oliveira Lima: "Manuel de Oliveira Lima was the first occupant of the chair that you granted me in your upper room." GARCIA, Rodolfo. *Discurso de posse do Sr. Rodolfo Garcia.* Rio de Janeiro: Academia Brasileira de Letras. *Text available at:* http://www.academia.org.br/abl/cgi/cgilua.exe/sys/start.htm?infoid=8478&sid=350 . Accessed: 17/02/2011.

190 VARNHAGEN, Francisco Adolfo de. *História geral do Brasil: antes da sua separação e independência de Portugal.* 4.ed. integral. São Paulo: Melhoramentos, 1948-1953, p.307.

Finally, it is also important to analyze the eleventh chapter, written by Antonio Baiao, important Portuguese archivist, whose title is named *"Pau Brazil's Trade "*. What we see again in the *History of Portuguese Colonization in Brazil,* by analyzing the chapter written by Antonio Baiao, was the recurrence of the use of sources previously handled by other authors.

In a discussion about the name that Pedro Alvares Cabral would have given the land he had discovered, Baiao argued that Cabral called the new land 'Vera Cruz', the name was later changed due to the will of the king of Portugal and renamed as Santa Cruz. More important to us than the data on such events is the document listing instrumentalized by Antonio Baiao to compose his argument. To support his arguments, the Portuguese author appealed directly to the third edition of the *General History of Brazil* and the 1918 edition of *History of Brazil* by Friar Vicente do Salvador, which draws our attention because both works were annotated or prefaced by Capistrano Abreu and Rodolfo Garcia.

What makes this text more interesting is that Baiao builds a kind of historiographical discussion between Viscount de Porto Segu-ro and Capistrano de Abreu. According to Baiao, "Varnhagen tells us that Cabral, giving the name of Vera Cruz to the new land, intended to celebrate the feast that the Church would celebrate. Capistrano de Abreu corrects him, affirming that by naming the land, Cabral referenced the cross of the order of Christ, which appeared on the flag given by the king himself in his time of departure."[191] Thus, although the data on the sources and opinions that Antonio Baiao, Varnhagen and Capistrano had about them, the phenomenon to be considered is that the historiographical discourse remained grounded in a given set of document that included, in addition to some other sources, the third edition of *General History of Brazil* and the 1918 edition of *History of Brazil* by Friar Vicente do Salvador.

Thus, the chances of certain sets of statements being made about the history of Brazil found themselves confined in the histo-

---

191 BAIÃO, Antônio. *O comércio do Pau Brasil.* In: DIAS, Carlos Malheiro (Org.). *História da colonização portuguesa do Brasil. Edição monumental comemorativa do primeiro centenário da Independência do Brasil.* Porto: Litografia Nacional/ Sociedade Editora da Historia da Colonização Portuguesa do Brasil, 1921-1924, p.318, 322.

riographical discourse constituted by the relationship - like a texture - between these texts. By the very nature of historical knowledge, that is, to be a discourse about the past built from vestiges, documents that serve as records of information of a particular preterit reality, although such traces constitute contemporary objects to historians, considering that the past is before anything a quality of these objects as discussed above, it was like it seemed hardly possible for the authors in question to develop of a virtually possible divergent historiographical discourse by combining quite similar set of sources known until then.

In one of his pages, Antonio Baiao wrote that "The Regiment of *the Bretoa Ship* was made known for the 1st time in 1844 by Varnhagen and then published in Note 13 (pp. 427-432) of the 1st volume of HGB, 1st edition. In 1861 was published in Volume XXIV, 1st trimester, the *RIHGB* and, in 1858, it had already been published, although very incorrectly, in *Historical Chorographia* of Mello Moraes."[192] As we can see, the same document was published four times in different works, two by Varnhagen, if not considered other issues of *General History of Brazil*. However, in addition to considering such amount of editions, it is important to observe that this document was still relevant during the first three decades of the twentieth century, offering valuable historical information in order to answer the historians' questions. This does not mean such a document was essential for constituting a narrative about the history of Brazil or that there were no other appropriate or important documents. Rather, the question should be asked in another way, which means we shall think about how the recurrent set of documents discussed above was related and organized in a historiographical narrative built according to the national point of view. Those historians could not avoid studying this set of sources and structuring their narratives as "national history" because although documents were apparently scarce, the most restrictive part of this historiographical machinery was played by the narrative national point of view and some specific theoretical choices.

---

192 BAIÃO, Antônio. *O comércio do Pau Brasil*. In: DIAS, Carlos Malheiro (Org.). *História da colonização portuguesa do Brasil. Edição monumental comemorativa do primeiro centenário da Independência do Brasil*. Porto: Litografia Nacional/ Sociedade Editora da Historia da Colonização Portuguesa do Brasil, 1921-1924, p.334.

Exactly due to being included in that discursive conformation, Capistrano can say that Brazilian history and historiography depended fundamentally on the "tracking and rigorous investigation of the sources, indicating the gaps, discussing the facts narrated by their predecessor and, finally, the comprehensive Bibliographic annotation of contemporary documents and recent monographs on the theme concerned", thus the inclusion of the "body of creative doctrines that in recent years constituted in science under the name of sociology" in the historiographical production process, which by that time was a more radical option of theoretical innovation of the Brazilian history and historiography.[193] The lack of sociological thought in the work of Varnhagen was so even considered by Capistrano as a major fault on the part of the Viscount. [194] On the other hand, that is the reason why *General History of Brazil* persisted as the main core of valid statements regarding "National History " for so long, being referenced in works produced for about half a century after his death.[195]

Thus, we are faced once again with Capistrano's findings about the founding function of Brazilian historiography exercised by Varnhagen. It was the Viscount who has not only accumulated "the Cyclopean mass of material" he had used in his narrative, as also he who "has always sought and often managed to put himself under the actual national point of view."[196] That is, after Varnhagen there was not someone who could discover, and handle such a set of original primary documents, as there was not for a long time, someone who could tell the story of Brazil according to the desired "national perspective" as did Varnhagen. At least there was no such recognition by academic peers and the public at large. However, this does not mean that in-

---

193 OLIVEIRA, Maria da Glória. *Crítica, método e escrita da história em João Capistrano de Abreu (1853-1927)*. Dissertação de Mestrado. Orientador: Prof. Dr. Temístocles Cezar. Porto Alegre: UFRGS, IFCH - Departamento de História, Programa de Pós-Graduação em História, 2006, p.104-105.
194 ABREU, J. Capistrano de. *Ensaios e estudos: (crítica e história)*. 1. série. Rio de Janeiro: Sociedade Capistrano de Abreu, 1931, p.135, 139.
195 GUIMARÃES, Lúcia M. Paschoal. *Da escola palatina ao silogeu: Instituto Histórico e Geográfico Brasileiro (1889-1938)*. Rio de Janeiro: Museu da República, 2007, p.79-90.
196 ABREU, J. Capistrano de. *Ensaios e estudos: (crítica e história)*. 1. série. Rio de Janeiro: Sociedade Capistrano de Abreu, 1931, p.135, 139.

novation, acclaimed productions or diverging speeches were not possible. It means, however, that the Viscount's "iron frames" imposed boundaries and guidelines in the discourse on the history of Brazil so that new stories of Brazil were narrated preferably according to the assumptions that substantiated it and continued basing and perpetuating the historiography subsequent to his death.

So if Varnhagen wrote his history of Brazil based on a wide range of primary documents and guiding his perspective from the point of view of national history, supported on a concept of procedural history conditioned by specific purpose, namely, the formation of the Brazilian national State, also the editors of the *History of Portuguese Colonization in Brazil* did it. *Thus, in the annotation process of the General History of Brazil* held by Capistrano de Abreu and Rodolfo Garcia, the "Monumental Edition" of the *History of Portuguese Colonization in Brazil* appears operating an important role of rectifying the historical discourse of the "monument" erected by Varnhagen, sharing huge similarities such as the sources chosen, the national *guiding perspective* as well as on the concept of history observed in the two works.

Used repeatedly in the critical annotation of *General History*, the *History of Colonization* was an important reference to contribute for Varnhagen's work to remain "alive" for almost one hundred years since its first edition in 1854 until the fourth edition critically annotated by Rodolfo Garcia in 1953.Since then, the Viscount's matrix permeated the discipline of history of Brazil, even many years after its realization. Reinforced by the rectification work operated by the critical annotation process of *General History of Brazil* done by Capistrano and Garcia, and under the epithet of "official history", "Varnhagen's ideas on the subject [the history of Brazil] continued to dominate the historiography, the pedagogically vulgarized historical knowledge and the political symbolism until the 1930s", during which also occurred an intense appeal to nationality and ideas of nation.[197]

---

197 Wehling Arno's .*State, history, memory: Varnhagen and the construction of national identity*. Rio de Janeiro: New Frontier, 1999, p.174, 193; "On the side of Brazil, the New Getulio Vargas State also stressed the seed and special links with the 'old and glorious nation' in which, in the words of Fontes, competed 'both the impulses of feeling, as deep reasons related policies the understanding of vital mutual interests of the two countries'. Almost two decades after the Centennial of Independence and the issue of *HCP [History of Colonization Portu-*

However, a last question arises. Whereas "the period of the late nineteenth century to the 1940s, more specifically "the decades of the late nineteenth century and early twentieth", were central to "the establishment of a written National history, in Brazil and in Portugal" as well as "for the consolidation of national identities in Brazil and Portugal", we must ask ourselves about the relationship between the *General History of Brazil*, the *History of Portuguese Colonization in Brazil* and their constitutional processes histories and national identities reflecting especially on the role of the Brazilian colonial past and historiographical accounts of the period in the two "monumental" works in question.[198]

According to Jorge Alves, the *History of Portuguese Colonization* "operates in a dual situation" in which it stood both as "the result of a particular political-cultural context, marked by emphasis on discourse on the nation and nationality", and as "linked in a particular aspect of this context to the inclusion of Portuguese-Brazilian memory within Brazilian history."

> This is a monumental work, a functional place of memory, in which Brazil is celebrated as a construction of Portugal and at the same time, it builds a recovery image of the Portuguese immigrant in which the colonial enterprise is actualized again. It is the private element that is responsible for providing the resources for researching, writing and editing the work and, in this sense, it also becomes a tool of munificence and power of Portuguese elites in Rio de Janeiro. These intellectual and economic circles, committed to social conservatism, usually presented themselves as the "real Portugal" as opposed to the chronic situation of political and economic instability experienced by the Portuguese Republic the 10's and 20's.[199]

---

guese of Brazil], the official political discourse positively contemplated the idea of brotherhood and the permanence of the Luso-Brazilian ties Concerted in 1922 ".ALVES, Jorge Luís dos Santos. *Malheiro Dias e o luso-brasileirismo: um estudo de caso das relações culturais Brasil-Portugal.* Tese de Doutorado. Orientadora: Profa. Dra. Lúcia Maria Bastos Pereira das Neves. Rio de Janeiro: Universidade do Estado do Rio de Janeiro/Programa de Pós-graduação em História, 2009, p.273.

198 GOMES, Ângela de Castro. *A República, a história e o IHGB.* Belo Horizonte: Argvmentvm, 2009, p.85, 95.

199 ALVES, Jorge Luís dos Santos. A memória do lusobrasileirismo na historiografia brasileira: a "História da Colonização Portuguesa do Brasil. *Anais, Programa e Resumos da XXVI Reunião Anual da Sociedade Brasileira de Pesquisa Histórica.* Rio de Janeiro, 2006. http://sbph.org/reuniao/26/trabalhos/Jorge%20Luis%20

Thus, the narrative of the *History of Portuguese Colonization* built a booster speech to the image of Portugal, under which Brazil's colonization process would be inserted due to its exemplary character, as the great success of Portugal as a European metropolis at the forefront of propagating its "civilization" in the world. "In short, the division of the collection indicated the intention of narrating the genesis of the Brazilian nation, according to the view that the Portuguese 'traditional nationalism' replicated in America what it had performed in Europe."[200] Such fundamentally positive speech about the Portuguese colonization of Brazil was constituted under three guidelines: "registering in a big way the place of Portugal in the formation of the Brazilian nation"; "Emphasizing the presence of the Portuguese immigrant, whose work was equated with the former colonizers and explorers of the colonial period"; claiming "to the modern Portuguese explorer - the immigrant - a space in the Brazil of the twentieth century." This appreciation of the Portuguese colonization of Brazil, was articulated not only by the discursive valuation of the Portuguese -Brazilianism and Portuguese immigrants living in Brazil in the early twentieth century, but also, and in a unique way, by the idea that "a nation with a small population and lack of economic resources maintained, and could still maintain, a colonial empire", justifying contemporary discussions about the possibility of Portugal to keep its African colonies.[201]

However, what concerns us more prominently was that, through the numerous texts of the three volumes of the *History of Portuguese Colonization in Brazil,* especially those written by Carlos Malheiro Dias, a great appreciation of discourse of Brazilian colonial heritage of Portuguese work was stated in convergence with the discourse cons-

---

Santos%20Alves.pdf. Accessed on 18/05/2010.

200 ALVES, Jorge Luís dos Santos. *Malheiro Dias e o luso-brasileirismo: um estudo de caso das relações culturais Brasil-Portugal.* Tese de Doutorado. Orientadora: Profa. Dra. Lúcia Maria Bastos Pereira das Neves. Rio de Janeiro: Universidade do Estado do Rio de Janeiro/Programa de Pós-graduação em História, 2009, p.286.

201ALVES, Jorge Luís dos Santos. A memória do lusobrasileirismo na historiografia brasileira: a "História da Colonização Portuguesa do Brasil. *Anais, Programa e Resumos da XXVI Reunião Anual da Sociedade Brasileira de Pesquisa Histórica.* Rio de Janeiro, 2006.http://sbph.org/reuniao/26/trabalhos/Jorge%20Luis%20 Santos%20Alves.pdf. Accessed on 18/05/2010.

tructed by Varnhagen in the *General History of Brazil,* and reaffirmed through multiple footnotes introduced by Capistrano de Abreu and Rodolfo Garcia during the critical annotation process of that work.

Despite the differences regarding political and social projects that supported the production of the *General History of Brazil* and *History of Portuguese Colonization in Brazil,* and despite the significant period of time that separates the publication of the two works, the discourse on Brazilian colonial history remained founded on some elements already highlighted earlier, namely: the great appreciation of the use of primary documents, especially those deposited in archives; the orientation of the narrative from the perspective of national history; the conception that the colonial past was the crucial period in the history of the nation and the Brazilian nationality, which would thus fundamentally exist due to the Portuguese colonizing action.

The divergence between the discourses arises, however, when they are under actualization process. That is, if on one hand the colonial past is characterized as the glory of the Portuguese State and thus is transferred to the Portuguese national history, and likely even to be related to the political and social projects in the Portugal of the early twentieth century, on the other hand, the same elements that underlie such discourse are updated strictly according to the discursive construction that integrates and transform the colonial past of Portuguese America into Brazilian "National history", relating to the conformation of projects in the history of the Brazilian territory, nationality and State. As we have argued, this process was developed from the mid-nineteenth century, when *the General History of Brazil* was first published still during the Empire, until the initial decades of the twentieth century, a period in which the work was more than once noted, edited and published, then under the republican regime.[202] Given this situation, the history of the Brazilian colonial period was disputed, exchanged, covenanted and spread between two historiographical discourses of nationalist background, though not necessarily nationalists regarding the same nation. It was the "National History" between two "monuments".

---

202 CEZAR, Temístocles. A geografia servia, antes de tudo, para unificar o Império: escrita da história e saber geográfico no Brasil oitocentista. Ágora, Santa Cruz do Sul, v.11, n.1, p.79-99, jan./jun, 2005.

In the 20s, then, the reading of the HCP was made according to different perceptions about the nation and the existing nationality in the social environment. Intellectuals who were thinking according to "*lusófobo*" and "*lusófilo*" scheme of ideas, fought for the representations of the colonial past understood as the nation's origin and projected these representations, from the collective memory, in preparing a speech about the nation's history and its application in political strategies. (...) In the case of the *History of Portuguese Colonization in Brazil*, it is referred to as a monumental work, praised by the collection and reproduction of maps, documents and prints that places it in the national historiography, especially in Portuguese-Brazilian historiography. [203]

So until the mid-twentieth century, the history of Brazil written by Varnhagen was rectified by his annotators, representing a national history of massive diffusion, which spilled over from primary school to university.[204] This national history was fundamentally grounded in certain precepts analyzed to date: appreciation of the colonial period as a formation period of Brazilian nationality; an ideal historical reality potentially existent to beyond its possible representations regarding past realities of reference; the vulgarization of a history of Brazil that especially values aspects related to the formation of the Brazilian national state due to the effective resonances of colonial past.

Varnhagen's work became a paradigm in Brazilian culture in three aspects: its intrinsic scientific value; its role in the construction of a particular type of national memory; and strength in the development of an explanatory matrix of Brazilian history, that Capistrano calls the 'iron frames' of Varnhagen. The evolution of

203 ALVES, Jorge Luís dos Santos. A memória do lusobrasileirismo na historiografia brasileira: a "História da Colonização Portuguesa do Brasil. *Anais, Programa e Resumos da XXVI Reunião Anual da Sociedade Brasileira de Pesquisa Histórica.* Rio de Janeiro, 2006. http://sbph.org/reuniao/26/trabalhos/Jorge%20Luis%20Santos%20Alves.pdf. Accessed on 18/05/2010 at 15:10.
204 *Brazil's General History* of Varnhagen "would become a model for more than a century, not only to the political historiography, as to textbooks. They were 'iron frames' as referred by Capistrano de Abreu, who wished without being successful, escaping.from them "WEHLING, Arno. *Estado, história, memória: Varnhagen e a construção da identidade nacional.* Rio de Janeiro: Nova Fronteira, 1999, p.186, 216-217.

the assumptions made about Varnhagen's work can provide some indications on the constitution of this paradigm.[205]

Such "assumptions issued in connection with the work of Varnhagen" reaffirmed a conception of history based on the idea of a long collective temporal enterprise we know as history, process in which the history of Portugal and its colonies in America already foreseen the successes and the glories of the future national state. In order to write this story it was necessary to accumulate and review documents as much as possible, preferentially primary and written ones, existing in official archives in order to compose a historical narrative more "realistically true", since it was believed that the past and the history had a specific purpose and aim – a *télos* – which effective existence would progressively unfold itself through a time-long process beyond all the possible narratives that may represent such pasts and histories. Within this epistemological scenario, the documents appeared to suggest the possibility of an almost direct access to such preterit realities. They seemed to affirm and secure the meanings infused in such narratives, especially from the perspective of the state and the nation. Since 1854, the initial date of publication of the first edition of the *General History of Brazil* - until 1953 - the date of publication of the fourth edition annotated and revised by Rodolfo Garcia - the national history seems to have been confined within the "iron frames" of Varnhagen.

---

205 RODRIGUES, José Honório. *História da História do Brasil.* São Paulo: Companhia Editora Nacional, 1978-1988, p.195.

The founder of the "National History"

This last chapter will specifically address the question of how Francisco Adolfo de Varnhagen was discursively settled as the leading authority on the history of Brazil, by means of the critical annotation process of *General History of Brazil* held by Capistrano de Abreu and Rodolfo Garcia. As we have argued previously, there was the articulation of three basic elements that lead to Varnhagen to be considered the authority of the "National History", namely: primacy in the discovery, in the collection, editing and the use of a wide range of primary documents from the colonial period; historiographical narrative organized according to a national guiding perspective; historiographical conception that the history would seem to exist beyond linguistics representations that built it.

Therefore, we shall ask ourselves about the relationship between these three elements and the discursive formation process of Varnhagen as the great authority on national history. Therefore, we will discuss about the essential characteristics of the concept of authority and its implications. We realize that some other characteristics of the phenomenon of authority articulated up or remained as a basis for the triad of those fundamental elements that operated for shaping the discursive authority of Viscount of Porto Seguro. The functions and relative positions of Capistrano de Abreu and Rodolfo Garcia in a derivative hierarchy of Varnhagen's authority will also be analyzed.

Finally, the phenomenon of establishing Varnhagen's authority must be understood as involved and permeated by the disciplinary discursive formation process of the history of Brazil, since both phenomena occurred simultaneously.

The phenomenon of authority: the foundation, the excess, the duration, and the recognition

In the instigating text entitled *"What is authority"*, the philosopher Hannah Arendt established some key features on the concept of authority, which will be discussed below. However, it should be emphasized that Arendt begins her essay warning us that the question posed in the title should be another: not what is authority, but, what was the authority. According to Arendt, the authority would have disappeared from the modern world due to "a constant crisis of authority, always growing ever deeper, that followed the development of the modern world in our [twentieth] century." However, the author did not give up on formulating a definition of authority, which, according to Arendt, could be understood "a-historically", that is, although this concept is built on a foundation of certain historical experiences. It has content, a nature and a defined function that can be understood by us today, despite the alleged vanishing phenomenon of authority in our modern world.[206]

Still according to the author, the crisis of authority was originally and essentially political, once the political movements and the forms of totalitarian government that emerged during the first half of the twentieth century, were, more a symptom of our loss of authority, than a result of the actions of totalitarian governments. The ruin "more or less general and more or less dramatic of all traditional authorities" was the great enabling substrate of the widespread occurrence of totalitarian governments from the early twentieth century. However, the crisis of authority did not remain restricted to the sphere of political phenomena, having just been the "most significant symptom of the crisis, indicating its depth and seriousness". Its dissemination "to pre-political areas such as child-rearing and education", in which the authority had always been understood as necessary and natural. It was through the basic political need of continuing an established civilization, "that can only be guaranteed if those who have recently arrived into this world are guided through a pre-set world in which they were born as foreigners," the phenomenon and the concept of authority acquired its strengths and its structuring capacity of a common world.[207]

Regarding Hannah Arendt, we would not be able to really know what would be the authority anymore, "both practically and theoretically," her reflection on authority had to be presented, therefore, as a proposal to "reconsider what authority was historically and

---

206 ARENDT, Hannah. *Que é Autoridade?* In: *Entre o passado e o futuro*. São Paulo: Perspectiva, 2007, p.127-128, 141-142.

207 ARENDT, Hannah. *Que é Autoridade?* In: *Entre o passado e o futuro*. São Paulo: Perspectiva, 2007,.p.128.

the sources of its strength and significance "because according to the author, the authority, that was lost and in crisis within the modern world would not be the" 'general authority', but rather a very specific form, which was valid throughout the Western world for a long period of time." For Arendt, it is important to discuss at the beginning, some observations regarding what the authority was not. According to the author, the authority should not be confused with notions of power, violence, coercion, persuasion or argument. "If the concept of authority should be defined in any way, it must be, then, as opposed to both: coercion by force and persuasion through arguments."[208]

Thus, Arendt argues that the concept of authority on which she reflects is based in two old, but diverse, concepts of what it meant or could have meant the concept of authority. On the one hand we had the Greek formulation, more diffuse, of Platonic and Aristotelian origin, possibly drawn from the time when Plato and Aristotle began to consider an "alternative to the usual Greek way of handling domestic affairs, which was through persuasion (*peithein)*, as well as the common method of treating foreign affairs, which was through force and violence (*bía)*". According to the author, "the word and the concept are of Roman origin. Neither the Greek nor the various political experiences of Greek history show any knowledge of the concept of authority nor of the type of government it implies." Thus, Hannah Arendt argues that the formulation of the concept of authority would be Roman and would rest "exclusively in the past, on the foundation of Rome and the greatness of the ancestors."[209]

Due to this kind of lack of political experience able to support the constitution of the concept of authority among the Greeks, such a concept would have been formulated in a diffuse manner, based on a set of experiences that diverged from the ones of the Roman case.

---

208 ARENDT, Hannah. *Que é Autoridade?* In: *Entre o passado e o futuro.* São Paulo: Perspectiva, 2007,p.129.

209 ARENDT, Hannah. *Que é Autoridade?* In: *Entre o passado e o futuro.* São Paulo: Perspectiva, 2007,p.129-130, 136, 142, 180-181; "When the historian Dion Cassius notes that the Greek language knows no equivalent of *auctoritas,* and it is almost impossible to find it a univocal translation, which has validity 'in a definitive way', suggests that perhaps the Greeks came to Similar experiences in various fields, but that did not work out with this generality, a notion of order, "that is, as the Roman notion of authority. Revault D'Allonnes, Myriam. *El poder de los comienzos. Ensayo sobre la autoridad.Buenos Aires: Amorrortu, 2008,* p.30.

The sphere of household and family life management, in which the householder should rule his house as a "despot" was the basis for the formulation of the concept of authority among the Greeks, mainly outlined by the political philosophy of Plato and Aristotle. Therefore, For the Greeks, the phenomenon of authority was thought through conceptual prototypes that emerged from the reflection on certain kinds of authoritarian relationships such as those between the doctor and the patient, the expert and the layman, the shepherd and the flock or the educator and the student. Still, despite the lack of a set of political experiences capable of providing the formulation of the concept of authority as done by the Romans, "the political philosophies of Plato and Aristotle have dominated all subsequent political thought, even when their concepts have overshadowed the political experiences as diverse as those of the Romans. "[210]

However, for the Romans, the essence of authority was the foundation. If the Greeks could say, in times of crisis, "Go and found a new city because wherever you are it will be always a *polis*" for the Romans, the foundation of Rome had sacredness, and new cities were only founded in order to increase the limits of the city. Once something was founded, the preservation of such a thing would remain as a capital obligation for future generations. For the Romans, the foundation represented a single event, unrepeatable, only able to be increased or improved.[211]

Thus, religion, tradition and authority constituted a kind of trinity, whose elements were related to each other. To the tradition was reserved the role of turning natural to the young members of a particular community, the world order previously established by the old. "Tradition preserved the past bequeathed from one generation to another through the testimony of the ancestors who first witnessed and created the sacred founding and then expanded it with their authority in the course of centuries." Religion meant the act of connecting to the past, to the foundation (from the Latin: *re-ligare*). The word authority, on the other hand, derived from the Latin word *"auctoritas"*, which has derived from the Latin verb *"augere"*, meaning "to increase," and that is why what "the authority or those in its possession cons-

210 ARENDT, Hannah. *Que é Autoridade?* In: *Entre o passado e o futuro*. São Paulo: Perspectiva, 2007,p.143-145, 156-159, 180.

211 ARENDT, Hannah. *Que é Autoridade?* In: *Entre o passado e o futuro*. São Paulo: Perspectiva, 2007,p.162-163.

tantly increase is the foundation." Thus, the authority is intrinsically related to the past, specifically to the founding event, aggregating to every moment or singular event all the significance load of the founding act. Moreover, Arendt considers that the authority of the subjects of the present time is always derivative of older individuals and consequently from the emanating source of authority.[212]

An important element to understand the concept of authority presented by Arendt is that, the common point between the elements of an authoritarian relationship is specifically a hierarchic relationship in which the inequality between elements situated at different hierarchical levels is placed as natural and therefore not questionable. Therefore, the authority comprises a set of accepted and not questionable norms, which need to have a transcendent basis to alienate the contradiction and divergence from the hierarchical structure of authority. This transcendent foundation located outside the hierarchy emanates potential authority to all elements arranged through the hierarchical structure of authority. However, the authority of the element that is located at the top of the hierarchy is greater than those who are in the lower level, reducing their authority the further they are from the apex of the hierarchical structure of a particular authority relationship. And finally, another essential element for the creation of the concept and the authority phenomenon is the foundation, a founding event that enables the emergence of the link between the emanating source of potential authority and the element in the apex of the authoritarian hierarchy. It is the foundation that enables the emergence of all the derivative and hierarchic chain of authority.

Thus, the conceptual framework developed by Hannah Arendt to try to recover what had been and what may be the authority, was constituted as follows: The authority has a hierarchically structured operation scheme, in which the highest point in such a structure has potential authority relative to the lower elements of the hierarchical structure; each lower level of the hierarchy- or in a time-oriented scale, the most recent element - has a potential authority derived and smaller than the higher elements. Therefore, authority has a derivative nature; authority requires a foundation event which makes it dura-

---

212 ARENDT, Hannah. *Que é Autoridade?* In: *Entre o passado e o futuro*. São Paulo: Perspectiva, 2007,p.164-166.

ble; the source of authority is always a transcendent element of the hierarchical structure in which it develops through the elements that compose it; authority does not imply the absence of freedom but the restriction of freedom.[213]

Another study of fundamental interest to us is the thesis of the Russian philosopher Alexandre Kojève entitled *"La notion de l'autorité"* [The notion of authority], published posthumously in 1981. Inspired by Hegel's philosophy, this important text, arising from the author's reflections on the law and the idea of justice introduced in his *"Esquisse d'une Phénoménologie du droit"* [Outline of a Phenomenology of law], Kojève established a formal study of the phenomenon of authority, determining some types and essential features for such a phenomenon. For the author, a detailed and in-depth study of the phenomenon of authority was an essential first step to understand those phenomena related to the concept of State, especially in order to avoid confusion between the notions of power and authority.

Similarly to Hannah Arendt, although inspired by the Hegelian philosophy, Kojève also resorted to an understanding of classical Greco-Roman past and to phenomenology to establish what authority should be. In relation to what was the authority in the classical period, on the one hand, as seen previously in Arendt, we find the formalization of authoritarian experiences of the domestic sphere through the philosophy of Plato and Aristotle, and on the other hand, we observe the experience of the founding of Rome and the legacy of Roman law. However, the major difference between the two authors was that Arendt accomplished a study more focused on the conceptual content of authority, i.e. the historical experiences that shaped the concept, while Kojève, not neglecting such features, was more concerned with the formal structure of the authority phenomenon.

First, he highlighted what he named as the *"four* distinct *theories* (essentially different and irreducible)"* we "have been proposed throughout history", namely: 1) the theological or theocratic theory, especially derived from scholastic tradition, which states as the first and absolute authority the one emanated from God, and all other authorities, were derived and based on divine authority; 2) the Platonic the-

---

213 ARENDT, Hannah. *Que é Autoridade?* In: *Entre o passado e o futuro.* São Paulo: Perspectiva, 2007,p.134-135, 149-150, 187.

ory, according to which all authority emanates and lies on the notion of justice or equality; 3) the Aristotelian theory, according to which the authority is backed by the wisdom and knowledge, that is, the ability to predict and to transcend what is immediate; 4) the Hegelian theory, which, according to Kojève, reduces the authority to the essence of the relationship between master and slave or conqueror and conquered.[214]

Alexandre Kojève classified and established the essential characteristics of what he considered to be such a phenomenon through these four distinct and irreducible theories that would strictly correspond to the manifestations of authority. However, despite constantly postulating an essential character to the concept of authority he formulated, the author emphasized that "all these questions below cannot be more than sketches. I do not intend on stating a definitive and complete theory of the Authority. It is above all, about listing the problems and indicating the general direction of their solutions."[215]

According to Kojève, there would only be authority when there was the possibility of action and reaction, that is, there would only be authority when occurred the possibility of its non-existence, "the authority is essentially *active* and not passive". This means that "the 'real' basis 'of all authority would necessarily be an *agent*" free and conscious of its situation under an authoritative order of things. For the author, the *"authoritarian* act is distinguished from all others by the fact that it does not have *opposition"* by individuals who suffer the effects of this act. Thus, on the one hand we have the conscious and voluntary recognition of an act of authority, on the other hand, the latent possibility that the authority meets opposition and therefore denial, which according to Arendt ceases the phenomenon of authority since it does not imply persuasion or coercion, phenomena which both would allow the occurrence of denial or divergent action.[216]

To have authority there must be an agent and a patient, because the phenomenon of authority is above all relational, and necessarily implies a social relationship. According to the author, "the Authority

214 Kojève, Alexandre. La *notion d'autorité. Paris: Éditions* Gallimard, 2004, p.50.
215 Kojève, Alexandre. La *notion d'autorité. Paris: Éditions* Gallimard, 2004, p.55.
216 Kojève, Alexandre. La *notion d'autorité. Paris: Éditions* Gallimard, 2004, p.57;
ARENDT, Hannah. *Que é Autoridade?* In: *Entre o passado e o futuro.* São Paulo: Perspectiva, 2007, p.129-130

is the *possibility* that an agent has to *act* on others (or on another), without these others reacting on it, although always having the possibility of doing so." Thus, despite the possibility of a reaction act terminating the authority, such a possibility of reaction should always remain in a state of imminent virtual existence, that is, such a reaction should always remain as a potential, never escalating, since the very reaction to the authority destroys it, as soon as the existing possibility of reaction is carried out in a real way. Thus, Kojève establishes another essential element of the phenomenon in question: the authority needs to be recognized without effective opposition in order to exist.[217]

According to the author, the authority would still possess a legitimizing and normalizing character. If authority implies recognition and no opposition, it would provide consequent legitimacy and standardization, since the acts charged with authority would be somewhat predictable and even desirable, not allowing any real opposition. In this aspect, Kojève's formulation approaches Arendt's. According to Arendt, one of the fundamental characteristics of authority would be the fact that it is present as a measurement guide or regulatory standard.[218]

However, since every authority exists only through a social relationship in which there would be recognition and non-opposition by the subjected subjects, and considering that any reaction to authority is always virtually possible, it follows that all human authority would consequently and necessarily be perishable. Due to the essentially temporal characteristic of the facts and events relating to the human world, there is no real human authority that lasts indefinitely. According to Kojève, only a divine hypothetical authority would last forever. As the author proposes at the beginning of his book, such authority could only be represented as God, who academically speaking exists only as a concept and not effectively, what would bring us to the outcome God should be regarded only like an intellectual tool for philosophical reflection.[219]

---

217 Kojève, Alexandre. La *notion d'autorité*. Paris: Éditions Gallimard, 2004, p.58-64.
218 Kojève, Alexandre. La *notion d'autorité*. Paris: Éditions Gallimard, 2004, p.59-61; Arendt, Hannah. What *is authority?* In: *Between the past and the future. Sao Paulo: Perspective, 2007*, p.163-165.
219 Kojève, Alexandre. La *notion d'autorité*. Paris: Éditions Gallimard, 2004, p.54, 65.

In addition, all authority would require a justification or reason for existing, since it is precisely this reason that justifies its recognition by those who undergo it. In other words, we would be asking ourselves the reason for their existence and recognition. From there, Kojève describes what, in his words, would be the "four pure types" of authority. It is important to note that, for the author, each "pure type" of authority would match a set of theoretical formulations specifically created to address the phenomenon of authority according to certain parameters.

We will deal first with the *Father* model. According to the author, this would be the model of authority of the elders on young people, of a dead upon his will, of an author and his work, or, of tradition and those who hold it. Of scholastic, theological or even theocratic basis, according to Kojeve, this theory would be closely linked since its emergence and throughout its development to the theories that sought to justify the existence of God and the power of kings. Therefore, the authority of the father possess, as its main feature, the idea that it is transmitted *hereditarily*, as the authority of the father would be passed naturally to his son after his departure from a world in which both acted or could act. Thus, all authority of kings would be derived from divine authority, a transcendent foundation that would enable its free and total acceptance by its respective peasants. The model of the father authority is still the model of the traditional authority, because it is through reproduction that a community can establish its continuity and unity, even despite the fact that a lineage is partly a diachronic sequence of individual existences. The father's prototype would represent, therefore, the origin and foundation of a continuity to be perpetuated.[220]

The second pure type of authority to Kojève would be the model of the *Master* over the slave, whose variants could be, for example, the conqueror over the conquered or the military on the civilian. For the author, this would be the theory of authority developed by Hegel, and corresponds to the central argument that the master possess authority over the slave because of his physical or mental superiority, and during a direct confrontation that could endanger the life of the slave, he would prefer to submit to the master and acknowledge his authority than endangering his own life. "This is precisely why there

---

220 Kojève, Alexandre. La *notion d'autorité*. Paris: Éditions Gallimard, 2004, p.67, 81-88.

is authority: the Slave knowingly and voluntarily gives up his ability to react to the action of the Master; he does it because he knows that this reaction involves the risk of his life and because he did not want to accept such a risk."[221]

The third essential type of authority would be that of the *Chief* over his followers. For Kojève, this would be the prototype of the relationship of authority, which most characteristic relationship would be those represented by the relations between an employer and an employee or between a teacher and a student. In this case, the author elated such a model to Aristotle's theory of authority according to which the boss' authority would come from his keen ability to *predict*, to *guide* and to establish a *project* to guide the actions of the group. This model of authority is therefore intrinsically linked to wisdom, the ability to imagine what may come of the future. Those who submit to such authority do so knowing that its holder is always able to choose and act in the present, on behalf of future earnings. The boss acquires authority "because he saw *further* than others because he was the only one to have conceived a *project*", and those that the chief submitted, "would not have been able to exceed the level of the immediate data."[222]

Finally, the authority of the *Judge,* whose variants could be the arbiter, the Censor, or even the honest man. That would be the Platonic theory of authority, which would be closely linked to the idea of justice. According to Kojève, justice and fair laws would be the assumption of the *judge's* authority whose best expression is actually the authority of the *arbiter. According to Kojève, the arbiter has* the authority because their judgments should be fundamentally impartial, some kind of incarnations of a transcendental justice. The referee would represent the power of impartiality, objectivity, and detachment. The source of his authority would be so intangible, existing beyond the interests and actions of men, and therefore would result in pure and fair decisions.[223]

So after we have sketched said "four pure types" of authority such as suggested by Alexandre Kojève, it still would remain a last

221 Kojève, Alexandre. La *notion d'autorité*. Paris: *Éditions* Gallimard, 2004, p.68, 70-71.

222 Kojève, Alexandre. La *notion d'autorité*. Paris: *Éditions* Gallimard, 2004, p.68, 73-76.

223 Kojève, Alexandre. La *notion d'autorité*. Paris: *Éditions* Gallimard, 2004, p.69, 79-80.

question posed by the author, if all authority has a reason, a cause, a specific basis, how can authority arise or be transmitted? Thus, we meet again with the statement of Hannah Arendt according to which all authority should always be derivative. Curiously, Kojève demonstrated a congruent perspective to Arendt's, because, for him, there wouldn't ever be the birth of a new, singular authority, but rather the transferring of authority, "the same authority is already there (i.e. it is already 'recognized'), and this is nothing more than changing its 'material support' (human), by passing from an individual (or group) to another" so that it would involve above all a question of transmission or as stated by Arendt, of derivation.[224]

However, in order to explain the authority transmission potency, Kojève proposed a few suggestions. Thus, according to the author, there would be necessary to exist a permanent structure of the authority phenomenon through the parts of the continuing chain in which an individual acquires authority over its predecessors and transmits it to his/her successors, while would be also necessary a harmony between acts and desires of predecessors in relation to their successors. In addition, to enable this transmission, the authority must not be essentially linked to its holder, but rather closely linked to his deeds and works.[225]

Before moving to the analysis of the arguments of the French philosopher Myriam Revault d'Allonnes, which deals in greater detail on the issue of transfer of authority and the fundamental power emanating from the beginnings, we will address one last feature of the phenomenon authority according to Kojève, namely the fact that all authority is intrinsically linked to specific historical issues and temporalities.

According to the author, if all authority requires a social relationship based on the basic assumption that its phenomenal structure constitutes the relationship between at least one person who submits and another that is submitted, without the one who submits be taken to coercion or persuasion, and the one that is submitted does not show real opposition to the given submission, so all authority could only be a strictly human phenomenon, and thus essentially historical,

---

224 Kojève, Alexandre. La *notion d'autorité*. Paris: Éditions Gallimard, 2004, p.92-93, 95-96.
225 Kojève, Alexandre. La *notion d'autorité*. Paris: Éditions Gallimard, 2004, p.107-108, 110-111.

consisting of a necessarily temporal dimension. This statement that at first glance may seem simple or obvious, brings in fact fundamental consequences for the understanding of the authority phenomenon. First, if all authority is manifested along a temporal structure, every change of human relationships over time would imply changes in the authority relations in a given social structure.

> The metaphysical analysis of the authority phenomenon as led by Kojève, also implies that we consider it in a *world of temporal structure: the metaphysical foundation of authority is the time, understood as human time and history, since the authority is not a natural phenomenon, but social. The time has, therefore, as such, the value of an authority: the time has power of authority. But this does not only come in the form of the past, as it is believed most often, that is, the authority of tradition. [. . .] Each mode of time as such - past, present, future - needs authority's force. It is inserted in a movement of temporality: the past only has authority while it is historical (it's my past), future exercises authority only as a project, and the present is the time of action that records the memory of the past and the project of the future.*[226]

Secondly, each "pure type" of authority would be linked to a specific relationship between a given social organization and also a specific form of temporality. The authority of the *father* is linked, therefore, to the past because it is assumed that this type of relationship would be established specifically through the past character of the paternal function that leads to submission of those who recently entered the order of things in an already established world, i.e., children. Moreover, the *Father* authority is the authority that is connected specifically to a tradition. Tradition and the father figure are manifestations of the power of the past in the present. The authority of the *Master* would be backed by the strength of this temporality, as it was also assumed that the master acquires authority over the slave through the recognition of the latter that the first would be the holder of a power that would trespass and threaten the integrity of his own life. The *Master* authority is the authority of the presence per excellence because it is in such a model of temporal and social relationship that human actions possess greater immediate

---

226 Revault D'Allonnes, Myriam. El *poder de los comienzos. Ensayo sobre la autoridad.Buenos Aires: Amorrortu, 2008,* p.146-147.

impact. The authority of the *Chief, on the other hand,* would be based in the future precisely because of the foresight that the *Chief* should have to propose a temporally orientated project for human actions, that is, the ability to plan the historical development. Thus, the future acquires a virtual presence in the present, guiding the actions of people who were submitted to said authority.[227]

The type of the *Judge,* however, would be a kind of expression of authority linked to the denial of time. It would be the denial of time not because of the effective denial of any temporal characteristic of a social organization, but rather would be the denial of time precisely by the fact that a given society would value ideas considered eternal and universal. The predicate of eternity would not be bound to the authority or to a form of static time, but to the eternal elements considered in a given society, such as the perfect or exemplary actions and ideas. "Therefore, is not eternity itself, but the actions of *eternal* character that emanate authority" for a fair action "is out of time," not being linked to the "interests of the day", nor to partisanship "dictated by the past", or to "desires of future."[228]

However, we cannot put aside the thoughts of the French philosopher Myriam Revault d'Allonnes. Similarly, to Hannah Arendt, d'Allonnes introduces her important book entitled *"The power of beginnings: an essay on authority",* also questioning "what is authority". But it is important to note that if Arendt was concerned with the concept of authority according to a perspective in which the content of the concept received special attention, d'Allonnes expanded her reflection by adding a similar perspective to that adopted by Alexandre Kojève, i.e. to the author, the formal analysis of the concept and of the phenomenon of authority also proved to be necessary. According to Myriam, being the authority a substantially social and historical phenomenon, it is "universal regarding its concept and polymorphous regarding its figures."[229]

227 Kojève, Alexandre. La *notion d'autorité. Paris: Éditions* Gallimard, 2004, p.118-119, 125-128.

228 Kojève, Alexandre. La *notion d'autorité. Paris: Éditions* Gallimard, 2004, p.122-123.

229 Revault D'Allonnes, Myriam. El *poder de los comienzos. Ensayo sobre la autoridad.Buenos Aires: Amorrortu, 2008,* p.26.

According to d'Allonnes, it is commonly stated everywhere, from the academic and political spheres, to the spheres of education and family relationships, that we are living in a modern crisis of authority. However, according to the author, the belief in the loss of any authority within the considered modern time would be first of all a result of a naïve understanding of the phenomenon of authority, which would have as a fundamental cause the changes that we have experienced in our relation to time. "The authority is essentially related to time". Whether stepping into modernity our ways of relating to the temporal dimension have changed profoundly, consequently the way we understand and experience authority has also changed, even more if we consider that in modern societies, especially in democratic and liberal societies, there is the basic assumption of individual autonomy. The reason it occurred was the disruption of modern historical experience with the old forms of authority and the classical tradition as well. Therefore, the crisis of authority would be fundamentally linked to the rupture of the "thread of tradition", as suggested by Tocqueville, and to a deeper crisis of modern forms of temporal experience.

> "The movement of critical emancipation that characterizes modernity has made disappear all reference to the third? The proven loss of traditional ways of generating sense has only produced emptiness and meaninglessness? (...) Does not equality admit some asymmetry? In these conditions, where lies the authority if society gave itself the constitutive principle of its order?"[230]

Faced with such questions, Myriam d'Allonnes proposes some very significant considerations. Thus, the first consideration proposed by d'Allonnes was that the authority would be intrinsically linked to time, not so much because the concept and the phenomenon could be altered according to the historical and social conditions, but rather because the authority occurs in a world whose structure is essentially temporal. As the "space is the matrix of power ", "time is the matrix of authority". The temporal nature of authority would be linked mainly to its derivative essence - as previously noted by Arendt and Kojève - and it would be an inevitable dimension of every social tie,

---

230 Revault D'Allonnes, Myriam. El *poder de los comienzos. Ensayo sobre la autoridad.Buenos Aires: Amorrortu, 2008,* p.13-14, 22-23, 74-75.

constituting what the author defines as *public life,* i.e. what can maintain the duration of a common world. If the public space enables our living with our contemporaries, the *binding force* of authority, as well as tradition, allow us to stablish communion with our predecessors and successors, so that the duration of a common world would enable a kind of contemporaneity related to those who came before us or who may succeed us. According to d'Allonnes, what failed was not authority, but rather the traditional chains of authority: the basis of the authority would have changed.

Therefore, what the author proposes is that the authority is essentially linked to the forms of temporality: if it is the time that "has power of authority", if the authority only exists and is exercised when human actions are inscribed in a becoming necessarily historical, the alleged crisis of authority is related above all to a crisis of our relationship with time and the consequent change of modern temporality in relation to the forms of temporality experienced in the past. In modernity, the rupture with tradition, or rather the desire of rupture, led us to a view that the direction of human actions and social ties began to emanate from future projects. Thus, the author asks us if "the contemporary collapse of prospects linked to that of the future authority did not contribute to the crisis of authority". For the author, the question of authority should be placed above all from the perspective of its instituting power and its temporal structure.[231]

Regarding said sensation of losing social-historical sense experienced in the modern world, d'Allonnes argued that this phenomenon does not mean, however, the effective loss of meaning or an empty experience, but was related to the loss of a unit of meaning that can be shared among the largest possible number of subjects. According to the author, the modern man would be obligated to create meaning for his own world, since the chains of significance emanating from the past through tradition would be broken. Thus, modern man would live under the condition of a plurality of potential directions for life, and therefore, under a plurality of authorities able to justify and legitimize human actions.[232]

---

231 Revault D'Allonnes, Myriam. El *poder de los comienzos. Ensayo sobre la autoridad.Buenos Aires: Amorrortu, 2008,* p.15-18, 75.

232 Revault D'Allonnes, Myriam. El *poder de los comienzos. Ensayo sobre la autoridad.Buenos Aires: Amorrortu, 2008,* p.95.

Let us move to the characteristics of the concept and phenomenon of authority as exposed by Myriam d'Allonnes. The aspect proposed by Hannah Arendt regarding the essential hierarchical structure of every authoritarian relationship would be the very common element among those who exercise authority and those who are submitted to it. D'Allonnes argued that it would not necessarily involve a hierarchical relationship as stated by Arendt and Kojève, but rather an asymmetry accepted and justified by all elements involved in the relationship of authority.

> The relationship of authority, neither equal, nor hierarchical in the strict sense of the relationship command / obedience, implies certainly a characteristic *asymmetry:* a non - hierarchical asymmetry, if you prefer. Within the authority relationship, the two elements [minimum terms of a relationship] have something in common: they mutually *recognize* the justice and legitimacy of this asymmetry in which each of the parties has stablished their place "in advance".[233]

Because it does not imply a kind of relationship command/obedience in the strict sense, the authority can be understood as something that does not negate the freedom of those who undergo it, but rather involves a restriction of freedom of action. The authority of the founders is recognized and legitimated "not because they apply to the living an iron collar that was and must continue to be immutable, but because they 'increase' with their authority the strength of the actions of the living, which, on the other hand, will confirm the living experiences of their successors." "Authority does not command, it advises," it is "an advice that compels without coercion" or, in the famous words of Theodor Mommsen, the authority is "less than an order and more than an advice." Said advice is validated by the powerful meaning that the founding act emanates through the person who exercises the authority.[234]

According d'Allonnes, this "increase", so characteristic of the phenomenon of authority that is present even in the Latin etymolo-

---

233 Revault D'Allonnes, Myriam. El *poder de los comienzos. Ensayo sobre la autoridad.* Buenos Aires: Amorrortu, 2008, p.42.

234 Revault D'Allonnes, Myriam. El *poder de los comienzos. Ensayo sobre la autoridad.* Buenos Aires: Amorrortu, 2008, p. 28-29, 66.

gy of the word - *auctoritas, augere* - is in reality an excess of meaning inherent in all human action, but that, in acts and events that underlie an authority structure, survives the very founding act and provides a kind of long - term continuity for the production of new meanings related to the founding act. It is therefore necessary to consider another distinction proposed by Myriam Revault d'Allonnes. According to the author, "as well as the authority should not be confused with power, it neither reduces the tradition understood as a sediment deposit" because this kind of "sediment tradition" does not necessarily correspond to that excess of significance of the founding act which, before settling hereinbefore, allows the continuous production of a chain of meanings. The foundation implies first of all, the recognition of a prior meaning, i.e. the excess of meaning arising from the past in relation to the acts of a particular present time. And such excess not only enables the continuation of a chain of actions and experiences, but also largely determines the meanings created from a founding act.[235]

> "We recognize that the other is *superior* to us in judgment and insight, their judgment is an advantage for us, and has preeminence over ours. "The authority is based on an act of reason in which reason itself recognizes its limitations and the superiority of judgment and reason of others. "Understood in its true sense, the authority has nothing to do with blind obedience to a given order. No, the authority has nothing to do with obedience: it is based on recognition. [. . .] "Or, if you prefer, establishing a form of obedience in which men retain their freedom." [236]

According to the author, such excessive sense of authority structures would be linked in an essential way to the instituting power of acts or founding events, which would enhance the experience of the temporal *continuum*. "The strength of the authority connection is closely linked, ergo, to that interest in durability through the institution." Therefore, the power of instituting acts and founding events is only possible thanks to that said excessive sense of the founding moment.

---

235 Revault D'Allonnes, Myriam. El *poder de los comienzos. Ensayo sobre la autoridad.Buenos Aires: Amorrortu, 2008,* p.33-34, 95, 248.

236 GADAMER *cited* Revault D'Allonnes, Myriam. El *poder de los comienzos. Ensayo sobre la autoridad.Buenos Aires: Amorrortu, 2008,* p.68-70.

The instituting potential of the foundation in this way would create a stability of meaning able to maintain a world of common meanings, so that it would be possible to similarly experience the world by and among subjects of the past, present, and future. Shared world that the author defines as an *inter-est* (interest), as something related to an intersubjective structure. The introduction of a common world consequently enables a structural reproducibility, or rather a *generativity* of a world of shared meanings, as well as the phenomenon of authority.

> The authority does not ensure either the reification or solidification of the world, or the transmission of its experiences. One can say, that the sustainability of the world is not its stability, its inviolability or its immutability, but rather its *generativity*: its ability to be transmitted or its transmissibility. The *inter-est* [interest] is not only the intermediate space that - simultaneously - gathers and separates men: it is also the duration of that turns them on and off, unites them and gives them autonomy.[237]

Thus, considering that instituting power of the foundation, which enables the emergence of the phenomenon of authority, Myriam d'Allonnnes suggests that the recognition inherent in any relationship of authority - essential prerequisites for such a relationship, since there is no authority without recognition - implies mutually and necessarily the notion of legitimacy. "The authorization, considered on the axis of temporality, and no matter which way [whether regarding the size of the past, whether in relation to the future], it is a search for justification." And it is precisely from such reflections that the author states that "there are three essential elements that exceed the relationship command/obedience" and characterizing the phenomenon of authority, namely the recognition, legitimacy, precedence.[238]

Finally, we must bear in mind that the authority is strictly linked to a divergent temporality in which subjects who exercise authority would be located. It is within this other temporality that a subject or group of subjects was able to establish a given foundation.

237 Revault D'Allonnes, Myriam. El *poder de los comienzos. Ensayo sobre la autoridad.Buenos Aires: Amorrortu, 2008,* p.60-63.
238 Revault D'Allonnes, Myriam. El *poder de los comienzos. Ensayo sobre la autoridad.Buenos Aires: Amorrortu, 2008,* p.69-70.

Precisely because all authority implies a temporal dimension other than necessarily that of the subjects who exercise the authority, is that this phenomenon necessarily implies an *externality*, an *otherness*, that is, a transcendent dimension that assures a derivative continuity over time. Thus, the authority can be regarded as something "always already there", "an inherited obligation and a resource for action that begins," because it only increases what already exists.[239]

However, this does not eliminate the fact that there may be authorities whose emanating source is related to temporal dimensions of the present or future. As we have rapidly seen with Kojève, these temporal modulations only alter the way the authority gets its ballast. According to the French historian François Hartog, this process of institution of authorities linked to the future - a dimension of "not yet" as opposed to "already there" of the past and tradition, as also argued by Kojève and d'Allonnes - would essentially constitute the ways in which the modern Western civilization dealt with the great process of secularization operated from Europe at a first moment. Such authority of the future would also be related to the creation of numerous future projects elaborated by philosophies of history from the eighteenth century and gained strength throughout the nineteenth century: modern utopias of the progress. Regarding the kind of authority backed in the present, Hartog wrote that this is the typical form of temporality in which the founding tension between a "not yet" future and an "already there" past would be permanent. In this situation, the authority was sometimes based on the elements of the past, and sometimes in future projections, able to establish meaningful connections in relation to a particular reality of the present. Therefore, there would exist in contemporary societies, as stated by d'Allonnes, a large gap between what societies stablish and claim and what they really are or do.[240]

Thus, according to Myriam Revault d'Allonnes, every authority - considering that every authority is a historical and social phenomenon by its own nature - requires an act or founding event whose

---

239 Revault D'Allonnes, Myriam. El *poder de los comienzos. Ensayo sobre la autoridad.Buenos Aires: Amorrortu, 2008*, p.72-73, 190.

240 Hartog, François.*Ouverture: Autorité et temps.In:* Foucault, Didier & PAYEN, Pascal (Eds.).*Les Autorités. Dynamiques et mutations d'une figure de référence à l'Antiquité.Grenoble: Éditions Jérôme Millon, 2007*, p.29-33.

establishment is situated in a temporal dimension transcendent to the very exercise of authority phenomenon. Thus, the foundation would essentially be marked by an excess of meaning that goes beyond the specific time of the foundation and emanates such potential significance in relation to the subjects belonging to the hierarchical structure of the authoritarian phenomenon. Such excess of signification, re-appropriated and used with restricted freedom by the elements belonging to the chain of authority, necessarily implies the recognition of the authority of those who exercise it, since it would be through these individuals that the excess significance of the foundation would emanate to the other subjects. That said, if the recognition of the authority is still possible the continuity of a particular social body can be established and guaranteed over a time *continuum*, since the parameters of updating meanings that configured, has reconfigured and keeps continuously reconfiguring the said social body stays actively accepted by successive generations.

However, the emergence of new foundations cannot be eliminated as a possibility. Once new foundations appear, new meanings, new temporal structures as well as systems of authority are shaped, reorganizing the social body. Or, as well stated by the author, "what is authority but the power of beginnings, the power to give those who will come after us the ability to begin by their own? Who exercises it - but not owns it - authorizes their successors to undertake something new and unexpected. Beginning is starting to continue. But continuing is also to continue beginning."[241]

A historiographical project

During the first decades of the nineteenth century in Brazil, especially from the 1840s, it began a disciplining process of the history of Brazil. Related to that process was the production of the founding texts of history and Brazilian historiography, as well as the political and social process of formation and consolidation of the Brazilian national state. However, it was not enough to consolidate the state apparatus,

---

241 Revault D'Allonnes, Myriam. El *poder de los comienzos. Ensayo sobre la autoridad.Buenos Aires: Amorrortu, 2008,* p.253.

it was necessary to justify an idea of nationality that could be shared among Brazilian citizens. Due to this need, most of the inhabitants of the Empire were excluded from this process of construction of nationality. The nation that was being defined at that time, both in terms of political and social events, and in relation to the discourse prepared by that historiography, was shaped by modern European civilizational ideals, especially through a historiographical discourse that positively valued the Portuguese colonization process of the Brazilian past, that is, a nation formed mainly by groups of elites. "By defining the Brazilian nation as representative of the idea of civilization in the New World, this same history will define those who internally will be excluded from the project because they are not carriers of the notion of civilization. Namely Indians and blacks."[242]

To respond to such demands the Historical and Geographical Institute was founded in 1838, first under the tutelage of Auxiliary So-

---

242 GUIMARÃES, Manoel Luiz Salgado. Nação e civilização nos trópicos: o Instituto Histórico e Geográfico Brasileiro e o projeto de uma História Nacional. *Estudos Históricos*, Rio de Janeiro, n.1, p.5-27, 1988, p.7, 16-19; _____. *Entre as luzes e o romantismo: as tensões da escrita da história no Brasil oitocentista*. In: GUIMARÃES, Manoel Luiz Salgado (Org.). *Estudos sobre a escrita da história*. Rio de Janeiro: 7Letras, 2006, p.73; Ver também: CEZAR, Temístocles. The geography served, first of all, to unify the Empire: Writing history and geographical knowledge in the nineteenth century Brazil. Ágora. Santa Cruz do Sul, v.11, n.1, p.79-99, jan./jun, 2005; _____. *L'écriture de l'histoire au Brésil au XIXe siècle: essai sur une rhétorique de la nacionalité : Le cas Varnhagen*. Tese de Doutorado. Orientador: Prof. Dr. François Hartog. Paris: EHESS, 2002; GUIMARÃES, Lúcia M. Paschoal. *Da escola palatina ao silogeu: Instituto Histórico e Geográfico Brasileiro (1889-1938)*. Rio de Janeiro: Museu da República, 2007; _____. Debaixo da Imediata Proteção de Sua Majestade Imperial. O Instituto Histórico e Geográfico Brasileiro (1838-1889). *Revista do Instituto Histórico e Geográfico Brasileiro*. Rio de Janeiro, a.156, v.1, n.388, p.459-613, jul./set., 1995. _____. IV Congresso de História Nacional: tendências e perspectivas da história do Brasil colonial (Rio de Janeiro, 1949). *Revista Brasileira de História*. São Paulo, v.24, n.48, p.145-170, 2004. _____. Primeiro Congresso de História Nacional: breve balanço da atividade historiográfica no alvorecer do século XX. *Revista Tempo*. Rio de Janeiro, v.9, n.18, p.147-170, jan., 2005; MATTOS, Ilmar Rohloff de. *O tempo Saquarema*. São Paulo: HUCITEC; [Brasília, DF]: INL, 1987; MATTOS, Selma Rinaldi de. *O Brasil em lições: a história como disciplina escolar em Joaquim Manuel de Macedo*. Rio de Janeiro: Access, 2000; SCHWARCZ, Lília Moritz. *O espetáculo das raças: cientistas, instituições e questão racial no Brasil: 1870-1930*. São Paulo: Companhia das Letras, 1993.

ciety of National Industry, tutelage that was granted to the emperor after the institution of the 1851 statutes. Designed along the lines of the *Institut Historique de Paris,* the creation of the Brazilian Historical and Geographical Institute (BHGI) aimed to collaborate actively with the process of formation of the National State through the establishment of a historiography able to conform Brazilian history according to the characteristics described above. It was necessary to integrate Brazil to the group of civilized nations through the construction and dissemination process of a history and historiography according to which the genesis of the nation and the Brazilian State was inserted within "a tradition of civilization and progress," or in the words of the historian Manoel Salgado Guimarães, "the nation, whose portrait the institute intends to trace," should be made "as the continuation, in the tropics, of a white and European civilization." Also according to Guimarães, the Historical Institute has become "at the time the privileged *locus* from where someone could 'talk' about Brazil", role that was "legitimized within the imperial literate elite," contributing "to a progressive diffusion and homogenization of the 'national project' within this social group."

It is therefore the task of thinking about Brazil under the very postulates of a history committed to the unveiling of the process of genesis of the nation researched by the literati gathered around the BHGI. The face outlined for the Brazilian nation and the historiography of BHGI would strengthen, aimed to produce a homogenizing vision of Brazil within the Brazilian elites. There is, once again, a certain Enlightenment-oriented position chairing the reflections on the issue of the nation within the Brazilian territory - first, those who occupy the top of the social pyramid possess a certain enlightment, which in their turn would be in charge of enlightening the rest of society. (...) In the process of defining Brazil, the 'otherness compared to this Brazil is also defined. In a very particular process related to the Brazilian case, the construction of the idea of nation is not based on an opposition to the former Portuguese metropolis; on the contrary, the new Brazilian nation is recognized as continuer of a certain civilizing task initiated by the Portuguese colonization. The Nation, The state and the crown appear as a unity within the historiographical debate on the national problem. [243]

243 GUIMARÃES, Manoel Luiz Salgado. Nação e civilização nos trópicos: o Ins-

Regarding the core goals established by BHGI in implementing the project of constituting a national historiography, we can safely say that the work of collecting and publishing documents about "National History", or better, and specifically, the documents relating to the colonial past, was the basic step taken to achieve such a project. Later, there should be produced monographic studies on Brazilian history and geography. Finally, at a later time, although this was not explicitly stated in the first statutes of the BHGI, it would be the time to produce a fundamental narrative about the history of Brazil, "a general and complete history of Brazil". In addition, "as outstanding features of this incipient national history, there is the role of the national state as the central axis from which the history of Brazil would be read, produced within the restricted circles of the imperial literate elite."[244]

---

tituto Histórico e Geográfico Brasileiro e o projeto de uma História Nacional. *Estudos Históricos*, Rio de Janeiro, n.1, p.5-27, 1988, p.7-8, 13-16.

244 About the members of such imperial literate elite belonging to the IHGB, Guimaraes wrote "an examination of the list of the 27 founders of IHGB provides us with a significant sample of the intellectual profile acting at that institution. Most of them perform functions in the state apparatus, are those who follow the career of the judiciary after legal studies, are the military and bureaucrats who, even without university studies, professionalized and roamed a career of average bureaucracy. A significant portion of these 27 founders belonged to a generation still born in Portugal, coming to Brazil in the wake of the changes produced in Europe because of the Napoleonic invasion of the Iberian Peninsula. This experience will certainly mark the socialization of this generation, creating the principles of rejection of the ideology and practices of the French Revolution and loyalty to the ruling house of Braganza. If we take the criterion of social origin of the founders of IHGB, we can see similar phenomenon to the already studied by Jose Murilo de Carvalho in his work on the imperial political elite. The diversity of social origin - which leads us to question it as the sole criterion for defining a practice both political and intellectual - is, however, capped by a process of education according to the legal tradition of Coimbra, then training and career unit State. It is from this perspective that the reading of the Brazilian history will be forwarded by the Brazilian Historical and Geographical Institute ".GUIMARÃES, Manoel Luiz Salgado. Nação e civilização nos trópicos: o Instituto Histórico e Geográfico Brasileiro e o projeto de uma História Nacional. *Estudos Históricos*, Rio de Janeiro, n.1, p.5-27, 1988, p.9-12, 15; Ver também: CARVALHO, José Murilo de. *A construção da ordem: a elite política imperial; Teatro de sombras: política imperial.* Rio de Janeiro: Civilização Brasileira, 2006; MATTOS, Ilmar Rohloff de. *O tempo Saquarema.* São Paulo: HUCITEC; [Brasília, DF]: INL, 1987; URICOECHEA, Fernando. *O minotauro imperial: a burocra-*

The members of the Institute saw the process of collecting and publishing documents as an essential historiographical level since the early stages of its foundation. Already in 1839 the collection of documents regarding "National History" in European archives, was considered of great importance, especially the archives of Portugal and Spain, as well as the collection of documents within the country through "trips and tours to the interior of Brazil, in the expectation" that such basic documents for the writing of national history were then collected.[245]

> An important source to track this ambitious project is the quarterly magazine published regularly by BHGI since its foundation. In addition to recording the institution's activities through its reports, disclosing ceremonies and various commemorative events, the magazine pages were open to the publication of primary sources in order to preserve the information contained within them - in fact, a substantial part of its contents in the early days-, of articles, biographies and work reviews.[246]

After a considerable period dedicated to the work of gathering documents on "National History", especially those contained in European archives, Francisco Adolfo de Varnhagen published, between 1854 and 1857, the two volumes of his *General History of Brazil*. Although he was not unanimously recognized by and among his peers of the Institute at first, Varnhagen was later recognized as the founder of Brazilian historiography, as we have seen throughout this study.

Therefore, this study aims to contribute to the understanding of the question of how Varnhagen was established as a fundamental authority on the history of Brazil by specifically analyzing the pro-

---

tização do estado patrimonial brasileiro no século XIX. Rio de Janeiro: Difel, 1978.
245 "In 1841 is published in the Journal Rodrigo de Souza, an article of da Silva Pontes containing the guidelines that should guide the work of the institution in locating sources." GUIMARÃES, Manoel Luiz Salgado. Nação e civilização nos trópicos: o Instituto Histórico e Geográfico Brasileiro e o projeto de uma História Nacional. *Estudos Históricos*, Rio de Janeiro, n.1, p.5-27, 1988, p.21-22.
246 GUIMARÃES, Manoel Luiz Salgado. Nação e civilização nos trópicos: o Instituto Histórico e Geográfico Brasileiro e o projeto de uma História Nacional. *Estudos Históricos*, Rio de Janeiro, n.1, p.5-27, 1988, p.23.

cess of critical annotation of the *General History of Brazil* executed by Capistrano de Abreu and Rodolfo Garcia. We believe that within the footnotes of said work there are possible answers to our fundamental question, hence in that annotation process not only the main structure of the *General History of Brazil* has been enhanced by the production of a convergent historiographical discourse structured on similar grounds to those created by Varnhagen, as well as through the addition of new information, criticism, and reviews, whether they were historiographical or documental ones. Thus, the critical annotation process of the *General History of Brazil* contributed significantly to the discursive shaping of Varnhagen as the fundamental authority of the history of Brazil, because it engraved the recognition of the Viscount's authority within the text and discourse of his own work.

Along with the study of footnotes it is necessary to take into account the articles published by Capistrano de Abreu in the late nineteenth century, because in such articles is precisely met the theoretical and methodological conceptions that largely guided the annotation work of the *General History of Brazil.* As discussed above, within the articles" *Necrology of Francisco Adolfo de Varnhagen, Viscount of Porto Seguro", and "On Viscount of Porto Seguro",* published respectively in 1878 and 1882, Capistrano presented his conception of how should be written the national history, also establishing a critical review on the Brazilian historiography of the time. Considering the theoretical and methodological guidelines determined by Abreu on said articles the following can be considered fundamental features to be adopted in order to write the history of Brazil, such as the narrative guiding perspective under the concept of Nation; the need to discover, collect and review the documents related to " National History", so that a more complete history of Brazil would be written later; the production of monographic studies; and the adoption "of the body of creative doctrines that in recent years [nineteenth century] has been constituted in science under the name of sociology" so that it was finally possible to "generalize the actions and turn them into theory," "representing them as consequences and demonstrations of two or three basic laws" about the history of Brazil, "the *rationale* of our civilization."[247]

---

247 ABREU, J. Capistrano de. *Ensaios e estudos: (crítica e história).* 1. série. Rio de Janeiro: Sociedade Capistrano de Abreu, 1931, p.139-141; Ver também:

According to the historian Rebecca Gontijo:

> If the death of Alencar can be seen as the key that opened the doors of Rio de Janeiro intellectual world to Capistrano, it is possible to state that the obituary of Varnhagen opened him the doors of the world of the historians. Similarly, to Alencar, Varnhagen also suffered severe objections, which accused him of writing history "uncritically and without style", but praised his capacity as a "researcher of historical sources." Capistrano took upon itself the task of valuing the viscount's contribution to Brazilian historiography, referring to him as "National historian", "great example to follow and worship", "the teacher, the guide, the lord." [248]

So what we have observed is that within the discursive formation in question, the adoption of a national guiding perspective and the primacy of the Viscount regarding the discovery, the collection, and critique of documents related to the period of colonial history of Brazil, have constituted the core of what Kojève discussed as part of the foundations of the authority phenomenon, namely, personal actions that require a special talent or skill set by the person who exercises the authority and which is not possessed by others. According to the reflections proposed by Foucault it would be more appropriated to assert that Varnhagen establish himself as well as was established as a *founder of discursivity*. This means since his *General History of Brazil* was published the discourse on national history has been shaped accordingly to the fundamental lines of his narrative, or, in Foucault's words, he enabled "a number of analogies as well" as he made possible "a number of differences," which opened "space for something different from him" that, however, still belonged to what the Viscount had founded. What is certain is that after Varnhagen's *General History of Brazil*, Brazilian historiography remained inserted within this complex process of production and maintenance of statements that, although potentially divergent regarding their content and form, continued being determined by the disciplinary memory of Varnhagen's masterpiece until at least the mid-twentieth century. Discursive divergence was possible only

SCHWARCZ, Lília Moritz. *O espetáculo das raças: cientistas, instituições e questão racial no Brasil: 1870-1930*. São Paulo: Companhia das Letras, 1993, p.28-42.

248 GONTIJO, Rebeca. Capistrano de Abreu, viajante. *Revista Brasileira de História*. São Paulo, v.30, n.59, p.15-36, 2010, p.19.

if specifically related to the parameters established by the authority. The consolidated parameters of discursive and intellectual legitimacy used to structure both criticisms and positive reviews.[249]

In fact, much more than a form of control or an intellectual deadlock of the Brazilian historiography of that time, as represented by the famous expression "Varnhagen's iron frames" introduced by Capistrano de Abreu, the foundation of the Brazilian historiography according to the parameters introduced over the pages of the *General History of Brazil* opened space for future historiographical narratives. As stated by Merleau-Ponty, it allowed the emergence of an institution. An institution could be understood as a sort of symbolic "inter-world". "This inter-world, this concrete weave woven by the world of human symbols, this *ambit of the symbolism*, Merleau-Ponty named institution."

> These events of an experience that endows it with lasting dimensions, in respect to which a whole range of different experiences will have meaning, will form a thinkable succession or a story/history, or yet the events that consign me meaning, not as endurance or residue, but as a call to continuity, requirements of a future.[250]

In this sense, the *foundation of discursivity* as thought by Foucault, can be related to what Myriam d'Allonnes called as a phenomenon of *trans-temporality*, which means "the possibility that an inaugural event, a founding one, makes a 'second creation' possible, a continuous series", even if the successively inserted events in the series are different and do not have anything in common, either in form or content, with the founding acts or events. What matters here is that the logic expressed within the excess of meaning produced by the foundation can be recognized, re-appropriated and updated by the successive elements placed in the series.[251]

Even the criticisms, reviews, and corrections added to the work of Varnhagen through footnotes and end of section notes did not

249 Kojève, Alexandre. La *notion d'autorité*. Paris: Éditions Gallimard, 2004, p.94; Foucault, Michel. What *is an author?* Lisbon: Vega Publisher 1997, p.58-60.
250 Merleau-Ponty *cited* Revault D'Allonnes, Myriam. El *poder de los comienzos. Ensayo sobre la autoridad.Buenos Aires: Amorrortu, 2008*, p.231, 236.
251 Revault D'Allonnes, Myriam. El *poder de los comienzos. Ensayo sobre la autoridad.Buenos Aires: Amorrortu, 2008, p.243.*

constitute a rupture in the recognition relationship inherent to the structure of every authority phenomenon, but rather rectified and *increased* the foundation proposed by the author. Within note number four (IV) of the end of Section V reproduced below, in which text Varnhagen (A [as for author]), Capistrano (C), and Rodolfo Garcia (G), discussed the truer location and description of the place that later would become the city of Porto Seguro regarding its identification with the current city. In spite of the annotator disagreed with the arguments and conclusions proposed by the Viscount, his statements remained closely linked to the discourse about the "National History" established by Varnhagen through the pages of the *General History of Brazil*. The same sources Garcia and Capistrano cited as reference to counter an argument stated by Varnhagen are precisely those that the Viscount handled with excellence being repeatedly praised for it.

> Cabral, as for us, anchored further south, in the port between the Gorda headland and the outfall of Buranhem, or Porto Seguro River, sheltered from the sea shore by several sandbanks, which on the driest of them he executed the act of domain. - (A.) - About this subject the author of the *General History* has published a note within the *Journal of the Historical Institute,* 40, 2nd part, 1877, os. 5-37, accompanied by the letter of Pero Vaz de Caminha. The matter was then discussed by Beaurrepaire Rohan, Zeferino Candido, Oliveira Catrainby, Salvador Pires, and Ignacio Joaquim da Fonseca, this last one favorable while all others were contrary to the Viscount point of view. The author of this line also did not agree with the Viscount, as seen in his opuscule *The discovery of Brazil by the Portuguese*, Rio, 1900. - (C.) - In his contest Thesis - *The discovery of Brazil and its development in the sixteenth century*, Rio, 1883, Capistrano de Abreu already settled the question: <<The arguments handled by Varnhagen are all broken down by these two facts: the first is the tradition attested by Gandavo, Gabriel Soares, Anchieta, Cardim, and so many others; the second is that current Porto Seguro does not match the description of Caminha, as much as he wanted to turn a reef into an little island. >> -. (G.) [252]

---

252 VARNHAGEN, Francisco Adolfo de. *História geral do Brasil: antes da sua separação e independência de Portugal*. 4.ed. integral. São Paulo: Melhoramentos, 1948-1953, p.87.

It is interesting to note in said note that Capistrano and Garcia did not even questioned the reliability of the data attested by these documents: the weight of the tradition was invoked to legitimize their arguments, tradition which was founded specifically by Varnhagen. So, as proposed by Myriam Revault d'Allonnes, "consolidating, growing, and innovating have nothing of contradictory" because "every significant intention recreates within the sediment, a new meaning that deforms it and exceeds it". In another words, the criticism and the inclusion of new information in textual body of the *General History of Brazil* such as operated through the footnotes and end of sections notes constitute stronger signs of the sedimentation and reactivation processes of the foundational discourse based on Varnhagen's practices and historiographical discourse, rather than the disruptor of the recognition of the Viscount's authority by his annotators.[253]

According to Myriam d'Allonnes, the "requirement of rupture or innovation" so dear to projects conceived by modern subjects does not presuppose its logical and necessary accomplishment. "It is not the realization of the project that has to be taken into account, but the project itself", because "giving in to the illusion of self-proclamation" is "adhering to the rhetoric of modernity." Those who exercise authority authorize those who take the project designed by the foundation on. "Beginning is starting to continue."

> The "authorization" to begin something new enters the invention within a network of open meanings. And the need - to arrogate yourself the present - to approach, to *reconnect* with what came before - in order to ensure the foundation - does not stop in the subterfuge of repetition, which dissolves the living of the present into the past. (...) *Continuing is to continue beginning.* And from this reversibility comes the recognition of an asymmetry that allows us to enter the world, to inscribe us into it and start something. Thus, the fundamental problem is to link the authority to the initiative and to make evident that the faculty of beginnings goes hand in hand with the authority of the institution.[254]

---

253 Revault D'Allonnes, Myriam. El *poder de los comienzos. Ensayo sobre la autoridad.Buenos Aires: Amorrortu, 2008,* p.31, 234-235.

254 Revault D'Allonnes, Myriam. El *poder de los comienzos. Ensayo sobre la autoridad.Buenos Aires: Amorrortu, 2008,* p 84-85, 139, 147-149..

Even Capistrano criticism about a hypothetical adoption "of a body of creative doctrines" by Varnhagen in order to his *General History of Brazil* become more complete, so would be possible to fulfill the necessity of "generalize actions and turn them into theory" of the Brazilian "National history", can also be understood according to the logic of increasing the foundation. By stating such criticism, in any way Capistrano eliminated or denied the historiographical merits brought by the Viscount, but instead proposed an option that from his point of view would constitute a historiographical advance, an improvement from what had been established by Varnhagen.[255]

Thus, the annotation process of the *General History of Brazil* done by Capistrano de Abreu and Rodolfo Garcia not only confirmed the discursive authority of Varnhagen, as it also established the authority within a unified process, due to the essential feature of authority: recognition. The recognition and the institution of authority are concomitant phenomena, even if certain explicit acts of recognition may seem decisive. It is not possible to recognize the authority of an individual at first so one can later make use of the authority after his/her recognition. On the contrary, the recognition is intrinsically bound to the very phenomenon of instituting the authority potential to a given individual.

We should also consider that not even the sacred aura of the founding event is able to ensure the enduring structure of the foundation. "It must be installed in the actual endurance what was instituted in the pact" of foundation. This is why the footnotes and ends of section notes added by Capistrano de Abreu and Rodolfo Garcia to the *General History of Brazil* can be understood as collaborating to the process of establishing the discursive authority of Varnhagen about the Brazilian history and historiography, because they preserved and updated the fundamental set of meanings proposed in the foundation, in other words, the production of a historiography based in the use of original documents of the studied period as well as the orientation of the narrative guided by the perspective of national history.[256]

That said, we shall reflect on another constituent element of the phenomenon of authority in order to understand why such features

255 ABREU, J. Capistrano de. *Ensaios e estudos: (crítica e história)*. 1. série. Rio de Janeiro: Sociedade Capistrano de Abreu, 1931, p.139-141.
256 Revault D'Allonnes, Myriam. El *poder de los comienzos. Ensayo sobre la autoridad.Buenos Aires: Amorrortu, 2008,* p.99.

discussed above contributed to the establishing process of Varnhagen discursive authority. The big question regarding the authority is that such a concept and phenomenon imply the inquiry of how to connect the demand for legitimacy and its subsequent answer given in terms of belief. It means all authority assumes a set of common beliefs of a particular social body, which enables not only the recognition and legitimacy of the founding act, as well as the chain of derivation and maintenance of the authority phenomenon. This set of shared beliefs operates as a "deposit" of meaning and as a "measure" for the authority. So, let us return to previous discussions on the index character of historical documents/sources and the presumption of a lacunar history-historiography that would be the more complete the greater the number of documents used by historians.[257]

As previously argued, Capistrano de Abreu and Rodolfo Garcia believed that the production of a new general history of Brazil, more complete than its predecessors, and specifically more complete than the one by Varnhagen, should be built on the basis of a continuous work of discovery, collection, and critique of new documents as well as new monographic studies related to national history. According to the annotating authors, this would enable a better clarification of potentially existing lacunar spots, gaps within Brazilian history and historiography. The instance of the sixteenth century and the issue of the *Flags*, for example, was repeatedly raised by Capistrano and even by Garcia: "is it possible that there is no ambition to publicize some obscure point in the past? There are plenty of them, and each more important than the other."[258]

This concern of clarifying ambiguities of the past contains a belief that history would exist beyond the representations built on certain past realities. By claiming that the research of new documents on the history of Brazil, specifically on the colonial period, would contribute

---

257 Revault D'Allonnes, Myriam. El *poder de los comienzos. Ensayo sobre la autoridad.Buenos Aires: Amorrortu, 2008, p.121-122.

258 As stated before in the page 25 of this book: "The *Flags* were a specific kind of movement called upon by those dwellers labeled *bandeirantes* – Portuguese expression for "flag men" – in order to acquire wealth by making hostages of American Natives and trying to gather treasures like gold, silver, diamonds, emeralds or drugs". ABREU, J. Capistrano de. *Ensaios e estudos: (crítica e história)*. 1. série. Rio de Janeiro: Sociedade Capistrano de Abreu, 1931, p.199, 204-205.

for the national history to become more complete and less lacunar, the authors were not referring strictly to the process of production, critical review, and accumulation of historical knowledge by the historiographical operation controlled by methodical procedures. Capistrano de Abreu and Rodolfo Garcia were also concerned with the completion of a phenomenal structure which the authors seemed to suggest having actual existence beyond the representations of such events, even though these phenomena was related to a temporality that does not effectively exist, existing within a past dimension, whose existence is conditioned by mediations such as memories, reminiscences, celebrations or any sort of physical signs recorded in the world, whether they are critically and methodically processed elements or not. As discussed earlier, the past is first of all a quality, a characteristic of certain objects, ideas or any other kind of artifacts made by humans, which act or suffer actions and consequences over time The historian Arno Wehling argued over the Brazilian historiographical case that:

> Thus, there would be a full correlation between the ontologically preexisting historical reality and the product of the combination of the sources. Their eventual limitations would be due to the information deficiencies: for epochs or situations with scarce documentation, conclusions could be only approximate.[259]

This belief led to the view that it would be necessary to collect, compare and submit the documents to processes of modern historical criticism, as well as publishing such set of sources and their integration into a kind of major national historiography, even if such documents were related to historical issues considered of minor relevance or just tangents to the historiographical knowledge. The important thing was trying to get the entire historical phenomenon. Thus, the greater the volume of documents used, the more truly complete a determined past reality would appear to be narratively rebuilt, "illuminating" history to the then contemporary spirits.

Discourses are not only a form of mediation between a given reality and a consequent more or less appropriate language translation, but

---

259 WEHLING, Arno. *Estado, história, memória: Varnhagen e a construção da identidade nacional*. Rio de Janeiro: Nova Fronteira, 1999, p.142.

instead, discourses define the very conditions of emergence and existence of thinkable objects to the human cognition, including allowing their discursive articulation as a quite complex weave of statements. We could presume that the larger the set of available sources used within a historiographical discursive formation, the more it would allow a relevant appropriation of a hypothetical totality of knowledge and set of historical phenomena of the past. The very existence of the idea that historical past should have a necessary ontological structure, which gaps located along the structure should be fill up evince the belief that such a preterit reality would possess some form of actual existence within a time dimension other than the effective existence of the present.[260]

Before we proceed, it is important to consider that "language and history remain dependent on each other, but never get to coincide entirely". If representations and phenomena of the past do not ever match, as we have repeatedly argued, the belief in the actual existence of the past in the present might only be possible, in this case, by assuming that such preterit reality would exist in the historiographical documents, being directly accessed especially and only by these documents, which would work as *indices of past realities*. Documents only become documents when made objects of thought by subjects who perform an intellectual activity, historians especially. Therefore, they would not necessarily constitute the past realities they indicate. Documents are traces of phenomena that happened in the past, and the very persistence of such objects in the present indicates that the object is not past, but rather that the object has temporal and physical qualities referring to a time already past. When we choose which documents we should use or not, we are already within an active construction process of reality. When we select and critically work a document in order to use it as source to write a historical narrative, we are operating a displacement of such an object from its first set of space-time coordinates to another posterior one since the beginning of this process.[261]

---

260 As previously mentioned, "the object does not await in limbo the order that will release it and allow it to incarnate in a visible and voluble objectivity; it does not pre-exist by itself, retained by an obstruction contours of the first light, but it is positive under conditions of a complex relationships beam ". Foucault, FOUCAULT, Michel. *A arqueologia do saber*. Rio de Janeiro: Forense Universitária, 2009, p.50.

261 KOSELLECK, Reinhart. *Futuro Passado, Contribuição à semântica dos tempos históricos*. Rio de Janeiro: Contraponto/Ed.PUCRJ, 2006, p.267; CERTEAU, Mi-

Therefore, considering the documents would be able to enable a more direct access to the past, as it seemed had thought Varnhagen, Capistrano, and Garcia, we could understand that set of sources as *indices* of the past. According to Peirce a sign is something that takes something else to refer to a third thing. Thus, the conception we have of an object is a sign that connects the idea we have of that object and the object itself. And an *index* is a variation of the logical nature and function of a sign. Such modulation of the sign in the form of an index allows the sign to enable a more direct logical relationship between the referenced object and the conception that we have of it.[262]

This direct relationship could be experienced even materially. The historical document can bring not only linguistic records of the past. The sources used also manifest in its constituent materiality other marks from events and actions originated in a past period. The color of aged paper, the accumulated dust in the archives, the old spelling, noticeably different from contemporary, among other examples, would constitute species of signs which would indicate sensitive temporal wear, in other words, as if the noticeable marks of material wear within the documents were marks of temporal effect, indices of temporality. Such objects might appear to constitute, therefore, the closest possible point to get directly connected to events or realities of the past.[263]

Thus, it is upon this belief of a history that is partly merged with the past, which allowed the conclusion that the respective past realities would to be able to exist even beyond the historiographical representations historians create about them, that there could be developed the complex conception of an essential relationship established between the fundamental importance of the historical sources of the colonial period and the adoption of a national guiding perspective. I reckon might have been this phenomenon that allowed the recognition of Varnhagen as the fundamental authority of " National History" by his contemporaries, and especially, by Capistrano de Abreu and Rodolfo Garcia.

For an individual to be recognized and to exercise his/her authority there must occur an "adequacy between the claims, the rea-

chel de. *A escrita da história*. Rio de Janeiro: Forense Universitária, 2006, p.81-82.
262 PEIRCE, Charles Sanders. *Semiótica*. São Paulo: Perspectiva, 2003, p.74.
263 PEIRCE, Charles Sanders. *Semiótica*. São Paulo: Perspectiva, 2003, p.64-70.

sons enunciated by those who exercise authority and the reasons for recognition granted by those who are submitted to it", however, the belief that sustains the phenomenic structure of the authority is always "different and it is more than the set of these reasons; surpasses the sociology of motivation, and it is *experience* that forces the introduction of this supplement. The belief is before or after, been perhaps more original than the motivational set (affections, interests, reasons): it transcends them."[264]

Rightfully so, the reasons behind the discourses and intellectual practices of Varnhagen, Capistrano, Garcia or the authors of the *History of Portuguese Colonization in Brazil* may be at times different both in form and in content, because the belief that fundaments the recognition of the authority does not necessarily coincide with those reasons: belief is the "something more" that sustains such discourses, practices and reasons, "the 'belief' never has an univocal meaning", it "mergers more or less rational representations", " affective beliefs ", as well as ideas arising from our prejudices. "The 'credit' granted to the enunciative or institutional authority and those who own it, is not only founded on reason. Granting 'credit' to an authority implies a species of pre-concept (a prevention) favorable to it: is not a neutral act."[265]

However, in the case of the *General History of Brazil* annotation process the reasons for the recognition of Varnhagen's authority largely coincide, albeit some divergences and differences between motivational sets and beliefs as discussed before. On one hand, the main reasons are precisely the central roles given to historical documents related to the colonial period in the history of Brazil, and the adoption of a historical perspective based on the idea of national history. On the other hand, the belief that allows the divergence is the concept of history often identified to the past dimension of time, whose existence would have actual occurrence despite the historiographical representations built on a particular past reality. This substrate of shared beliefs is what enabled this particular epistemology of history, according to which the more documents collected, criticized, and used to compose

---

264 Revault D'Allonnes, Myriam. El *poder de los comienzos. Ensayo sobre la autoridad.Buenos Aires: Amorrortu, 2008*, p.173-174.

265 Revault D'Allonnes, Myriam. El *poder de los comienzos. Ensayo sobre la autoridad.Buenos Aires: Amorrortu, 2008*, p.70, 182-183.

historical narratives, the more complete and less lacunar would be such narratives.

As we have seen, this common belief enabled the colonial history of Brazil to be privileged over other historical periods. The historiographies not centered on the colonial period frequently were restricted in regard to pragmatic, political, cultural or even personal factors. According to the "opinions, censures and judgments issued by the committees in charge of judging the merit of books and manuscripts" to be published in the *Journal of the BHGI,* "the disclosure of any kind of contemporary document that could lead to questioning the monarchical institutions on the grounds of possible bias of the authors" were repeatedly censured and repudiated by the members of the Institute, although there were some exceptions.[266]

Even the *History of Portuguese Colonization of Brazil,* written just about half a century after the *General History of Brazil,* was still major centered on the colonial period. Some of the most recognized Brazilian historians brought to public light since Varnhagen's book had been published as annoted by Capistrano de Abreu and Rodolfo Garcia were devoted to studying the colonial period. Intellectuals such as Sérgio Buarque de Holanda, Gilberto Freyre, Caio Prado Jr., Sílvio Romero or even Capistrano de Abreu in his more original historiographical works, wrote on colonial history. Most studies presented within the History Congresses promoted by BHGI involved the colonial history of Brazil.[267]

---

266 GUIMARÃES, Lúcia M. Paschoal. Debaixo da Imediata Proteção de Sua Majestade Imperial. O Instituto Histórico e Geográfico Brasileiro (1838-1889). *Revista do Instituto Histórico e Geográfico Brasileiro.* Rio de Janeiro, a.156, v.1, n.388, p.459-613, jul./set., 1995, p.462, 514-520, 534-535.

267 GUIMARÃES, Lúcia M. Paschoal. *Da escola palatina ao silogeu: Instituto Histórico e Geográfico Brasileiro (1889-1938).* Rio de Janeiro: Museu da República, 2007, p.79-90, 115-125, 133-192; _____. *Circulação de saberes, sociabilidades e linhagens historiográficas: dois congressos de História Nacional (1914 e 1949).* In: GUIMARÃES, Manoel Luiz Salgado (Org.). *Estudos sobre a escrita da história.* Rio de Janeiro: 7Letras, 2006; _____. IV Congresso de História Nacional: tendências e perspectivas da história do Brasil colonial (Rio de Janeiro, 1949). *Revista Brasileira de História.* São Paulo, v.24, n.48, p.145-170, 2004; _____. Primeiro Congresso de História Nacional: breve balanço da atividade historiográfica no alvorecer do século XX. *Revista Tempo.* Rio de Janeiro, v.9, n.18, p.147-170, jan., 2005.

By this I mean that this belief in the actual existence of past realities, which would exist despite the representations created of them - the language records and multiple sensitive marks that persisted until a determined present time - enabled that the colonial period of the former Portuguese territories in America could be understood as Brazilian history. Colonial history was considered an essential formative period of the Brazilian State, nationality, culture, and society. Questioning this common belief that biased so many historiographical representations, does not mean that we are denying the fact that the colonial past has influenced the constitution of Brazil as a specific State and nation, but rather we should observe how this phenomenon produces a continuous identity able to hide the inevitable otherness of any kind of past reality as well as of all beginnings.[268]

It was precisely this belief in a kind of transcendental history that enabled the institution of Varnhagen as the major authority of "National History", because his *General History of Brazil* enabled the emergence of a shared idea of common world not only among his contemporaries, but also regarding those individuals from the past and with those who would come into existence. The history constantly produced as historiography allows the existence of a great common world not only synchronically shared, but diachronically too. Representations are mediations that enable subjects to open a common world, shared not only in space but also in time by the endurance, appropriation, and updating of such representations. "The world of representations, which differs from the real world, it is an essential dimension of social existence, linked to the symbolic structure of action, an initial and inevitable structure. The human acting cannot fail to meet with the symbolic, starting with this *always already-there* that is language."[269]

The present gets its cornerstone by a celebrated past. But also the past of the discipline History received its sacred ballast from legitimated historiographical works. The *General History of Brazil* and its

---

268 "As noted by Assis Chateaubriand, the great merit of Capistrano would have been understanding *Brazilianness* - distinctive property of Brazil and the Brazilian - translating it through his studies of languages and indigenous customs and also about the colonial history ".GONTIJO, Rebeca. Capistrano de Abreu, viajante. *Revista Brasileira de História*. São Paulo, v.30, n.59, p.15-36, 2010, p.22.

269 Revault D'Allonnes, Myriam. El *poder de los comienzos. Ensayo sobre la autoridad.Buenos Aires: Amorrortu, 2008,* p.58, 185, 230.

footnotes history represent just one case of national historiographic cannon creation among others, being the founding event of the Brazilian historiography according to the tradition established from this founding process. Also the differences between Varnhagen's historiographical practices and discourses suffered such otherness reduction through his recognition as the founder of Brazilian historiography. The characteristics of the historiography practiced by the Viscount that were appealing to his followers were overvalued over a background of potential divergences, which his annotators and critics also noted with great recurrence. All authority implies an externality regarding the elements of the belief that sustain it, and an essential otherness in relation to its founding event. In short, we can claim that there was a kind of "will" to abide to "Varnhagen's principles" by Garcia and Capistrano, as well as by other admirers. This "will" shall be understood as the motivational set ballasted over a substrate of shared beliefs.[270]

The *General History of Brazil* symbolizes not only a historiographical project but also a national project based on a historical identity. It was largely the project nature emanated from Varnhagen's work that established him as the great authority on national history and historiography, so that the *General History of Brazil* could become an *institution* of these instances, or, in Capistrano words, a "monument". By becoming an institution we mean that through the Viscount's work it was possible to keep active the process of social bond generation that gives any shared world inhabited by individuals their symbolic permanence in time and space.

> The institutions unite the concept and the course of living, the world order and the resources of action. And the chain of authorizations, indefinitely reactivated by new generations entering a world always *already-there,* particularly shifts in the order of generative temporality the series of mediations between the identity of individuals and institutional conditions that update their ability to act: thus, this series is converted into a live objectivity. This way, the authority may be studied from the perspective of a continuing world provided by the generational relief, under the condition that

270 Revault D'Allonnes, Myriam. El *poder de los comienzos. Ensayo sobre la autori-dad.Buenos Aires: Amorrortu, 2008, p.172, 190.*

it has been given the possibility of innovating to those who enter the world, that is, to renew the common world. However, this is only given to them through the temporal dimension of the institution, even as they strive to deny it.[271]

Regarding the Brazilian historiography, *General History of Brazil* has become an institution and allowed Varnhagen to be instituted as the authority of "National History" because in the discourse and historiographical practices that supported its production, the *General History* brought the structural elements of a proposal for a national historiography. As we noted above about the historiographical criticism established by Capistrano de Abreu, one of the main goals to be achieved in order to continue the national historiography development process depended on the effort of discovery, collection, critique, edition, and publication of new documents related to national history. Historiography that was nationally configured by the colonial period discursive historical frames, as it is worth to remember. Thus, the historiographical discourse present in Varnhagen's work, as well as the practices that the author developed throughout his historian career, have settled into a kind of historiographical project that was posteriorly followed, appropriated, and/or updated by other authors. As we have argued, this was the case of the object of study proposed here, namely the critical annotation work of the *General History of Brasil* by Capistrano and Garcia. This historiographical project also contemplated the colonial documents that they have also noted, edited, and published. Varnhagen had even previously processed many of these documents. However, we cannot overlook the fact that this project found its first reasons and principles in the statutes and practices established by the Brazilian Historical and Geographical Institute since its very own beginning.[272]

---

271 Revault D'Allonnes, Myriam. El *poder de los comienzos. Ensayo sobre la autoridad.* Buenos Aires: Amorrortu, 2008, p.76-80, 217.

272 GUIMARÃES, Lúcia M. Paschoal. *Da escola palatina ao silogeu: Instituto Histórico e Geográfico Brasileiro (1889-1938).* Rio de Janeiro: Museu da República, 2007; _____. Debaixo da Imediata Proteção de Sua Majestade Imperial. O Instituto Histórico e Geográfico Brasileiro (1838-1889). *Revista do Instituto Histórico e Geográfico Brasileiro.* Rio de Janeiro, a.156, v.1, n.388, p.459-613, jul./set., 1995; GUIMARÃES, Manoel Luiz Salgado. Nação e civilização nos trópicos: o Instituto Histórico e Geográfico Brasileiro e o projeto de uma História Nacional.

According to Myriam Revault d'Allonnes, the author is either the one who intervenes for the future when proposing something, or who acts from the past assuring something to the present. "The *auctoritas* always shifts along time: it is located simultaneously in the past, as a proposition force, and in the future, as an element of ratification or validation." Therefore, the historiographical project outlined and symbolized by *General History of Brazil* served as a guiding model for the historiography later produced. The prominent role given to documents related to the colonial past and the orientation of a broad, general narrative, according to the idea of nation was the founding principles of the historiographical project represented by Varnhagen's masterpiece, a project which was especially recognized as fundamental due to the criticism on that work, as we have seen were done by Capistrano de Abreu and Rodolfo Garcia through the footnotes they wrote. "The one who owns it [the authority] receives it from an instance that transcends him/her because it 'precedes' that one: this 'excess' authorizes the progressiveness or, more accurately, the generativity. In other words, the very *bond* of authority comes not only from the confirmation of the established, but also from its *instituting* force."[273]

The founding act of the Brazilian historiography through the *General History of Brazil* writing and publishing processes entailed an excess of meaning that was later continuously appropriated, updated, and reframed due to its historiographical project structure. Such excess of meaning emanated also from an outside dimension related to the founding of the nation in the historical sense. The substrate of beliefs about the colonial past previously discussed ballasted a historical project of nationality. Determined ideas about the Brazilian

Estudos Históricos, Rio de Janeiro, n.1, p.5-27, 1988; "With the exception of Mr. Capistrano de Abreu, there were no good summaries of what was Varnhagen and other ordinary works without any novelty or research or thought.(...) He had Not only found the monuments and fountains where they had [his predecessors] drunk, but found or seized new, as those same took what they lacked. And this is critical work, indispensable preliminary to any historic building, which from the beginning was mainly his, which prominently marks the place and role of Mr. Capistrano de Abreu in our historical culture. VERÍSSIMO *apud* GONTIJO, Rebeca. Capistrano de Abreu, viajante. *Revista Brasileira de História*. São Paulo, v.30, n.59, p.15-36, 2010, p.20-21.

273 Revault D'Allonnes, Myriam. El *poder de los comienzos. Ensayo sobre la autoridad.Buenos Aires: Amorrortu, 2008, p.30, 74.*

nationality were being conformed according to this set of beliefs and the historiography produced regarding it, such as the idea that the Brazilian nationality was owed to the Portuguese tradition. The emphasis given by Varnhagen to the Portuguese tradition concerning the colonization process of Portuguese American lands could be reframed not only by the discourses recorded in the *History of Portuguese Colonization in Brazil,* which represented the great interest the authors had in promoting an image and positive idea about the referred process, but also by Capistrano de Abreu and Rodolfo Garcia, who saw the Portuguese colonization of Brazil as an important step toward the their present formation of Brazilian nationality. The retention of the past was a fundamental condition for the projection of the future.[274]

In his *Examine de quelques points de l'histoire géographique du Brésil,* in which he discussed the criticisms made by d'Avezac to his *General History of Brazil,* Varnhagen noted that he considered his dedication to "National History" as a fundamental imposition of order over "the true chaos in which was found the History" of his country. He "did no history of America, gentlemen", but rather, wrote that history "of the civilization of Brazil by the Portuguese". Once the *General History of Brazil* has been annotated, criticized, recognized, and meaningfully updated by Capistrano de Abreu and Rodolfo Garcia, Francisco Adolfo de Varnhagen settle down the cornerstone and future basis in order to found a national history and historiography. Through multiple pages and a colossal range of footnotes and end of section notes, the history of the Portuguese colonies in America conformed the history of Brazil. Simultaneously, the discursive authority of Varnhagen on the Brazilian history and historiography was recognized and reassured. Since then, the Brazilian history and historiography kept shackled in the Viscount's iron frames, waiting to be set free around halfway the twentieth century.[275]

---

274 Revault D'Allonnes, Myriam. El *poder de los comienzos. Ensayo sobre la autoridad.Buenos Aires: Amorrortu, 2008, p.182.*

275 VARNHAGEN, Francisco Adolfo.*Examen de quelques points de l'histoire du Brésil géographique or analyze critique du rapport de M. d'Avezac sur la récente Histoire générale du Brésil. Paris: Imprimerie L. Martinet, 1858, p.5, 7*

Final considerations

The first edition of the *General History of Brazil*, written by Francisco Adolfo de Varnhagen was published between 1854 and 1857, consisting of two volumes. In 1906, said work began to be critically annotated by Capistrano de Abreu and Rodolfo Garcia. Since Capistrano passed away in 1927, Garcia took on this challenge at least until 1948, when the later also died. After the *General History* underwent such an annotation process, its total length began to count four volumes instead of just the two original ones published while Varnhagen was still alive. In short, the work of Varnhagen doubled in volume, and the new pages then offered were expanded specifically as footnotes and end of section notes. Within these notes, criticisms were established, new information was added, new studies on the history of Brazil were disclosed, and recently published or discovered documents were reproduced. In this process, the fundamental structural lines of the *General History of Brazil* were rectified and strengthened.

Through the annotation process of Varnhagen's *History* established by Capistrano de Abreu and Rodolfo Garcia we can observe the characteristics of a particular set of beliefs about the Brazilian history and historiography. According to this substrate of beliefs, historical documents held an essential and fundamental role in the process of writing historiographical narratives, as if the documents were *indices of preterit realities* that seemed to enable the most direct possible access to such realities whose existences would be potentially guaranteed despite the representations we built of these pasts. Consequently, such a set of beliefs also implied the notion of an essential structure for the history of Brazil that could be translated into historiographical discourse as a narrative record, which should be the more complete the more documents were used for the composition of such a narrative. Hence these documents were understood as *indices of preterit realities*, and thus potential instruments to achieve a total reality that no longer would exists, only accessible through their betaking features, it was supposed the largest amount of collected documents would allow the closest conception of the historical totality. In this case, the past reality of reference was the colonial past configured into "National History" and understood as the essential constituent of Brazilian nationality. The documents played a fundamental role - in the very sense of the foundation as a founding act - in the construction of representations regarding national history and historiography, which would be able to determine what was supposed to be Brazil and the Brazilians, because since documents are conceived as *indices of past realities* they would allow this sort of "touching" act of a past reality despite the representations created on it: all sources are material objects existing in a present time albeit their preterit time coordinate of origin.

We have analyzed some of the most cited colonial documents in the studied footnotes. Most of them were discovered, criticized, edited, and published by Varnhagen, Capistrano, and Garcia. What we have observed was the existence of a self-referencing movement of the historiographical discourse recorded within the *General History of Brazil* footnotes and on the studied documents. Such discursive movement contributed to ratify certain possibilities of making statements about the Brazilian history and historiography according to the model established by the Viscount. As we have seen, this model implied the privilege of a narrative guided by the perspective of national history, which configured the past of the former Portuguese colonies in America as Brazilian past and history.

Those were the Varnhagen's "iron frames": it was like Capistrano and Garcia prudently followed the historiographical advice of Varnhagen. This did not stop criticism or innovations to be made because they arose within the discursive framework of reference guided by the fundamental lines established by the historiographical discourse of Varnhagen as written in the *General History of Brazil*. Such criticisms meant more an increase of Varnhagen's authority than its negation. At the same time that Capistrano de Abreu and Rodolfo Garcia annotated the *General History*, they also prefaced and annotated most of the referred set of colonial documents, discursively determining the range of possibilities in order to enunciate statements about the history of Brazil, creating said circular movement of self-referencing historical discourse, which also reaffirmed Varnhagen's authority on national history, and so on.

Regarding the *History of Portuguese Colonization in Brazil*, one of the most cited historiographic works in the footnotes of Varnhagens's book, we observed that the authors proclaimed the monumental character of the *History of Colonization* as it was in close relation to the also monumental *General History of Brazil,* stressing its importance to the Brazilian history and historiography. Once more, this phenomenon reinforced the structural lines of the discursive authority held by Varnhagen. The main function exerted by the sources from the colonial period, the narrative guided by the perspective of national history, and the belief in a structure of time reality that would transcend the historiographical representations remained operative in both history books. Also we noticed a self-referencing movement of historiographical discourse between the *History of Portuguese Colonization in Brazil* and the *General History of Brazil.* The *History of Colonization* was repeatedly quoted and referred in the notes written by Capistrano de Abreu and Rodolfo Garcia, while the edition of the *General History* noted by them often appeared along the notes and references of the *History of Portuguese Colonization in Brazil.*

Even the quarrel perceived around the colonial past in the narrative of the two works had in common the recognition of Portuguese heritage as shaping the history and the Brazilian historical identity. In the *History of Portuguese Colonization in Brazil* this shared past – even if it was partly configured as history of the Portuguese empire inasmuch as its American colonies – never ceased to be also configured as colonial history of Brazil, although such past and history have been symbolically articulated in order to recover the former glory the Portuguese state and nation had had once but no longer had in the early twentieth century. Thus, the past and history of Brazil emerged as a special mean for exalting the Portuguese past and history.

However, one last question had to be addressed. As we have argued in the last chapter, Varnhagen could be recognized as the great authority on "National History" not only because of the recognition of two main elements of his historiographical practice and discourse, i.e. the essential function of colonial documents and the adoption of the historiographic structural perspective of national history, both backed by the set of beliefs in the existence of the past as an effective time reality despite representations we create about it, but also and fundamentally, because the *General History of Brazil* represented the history and historiography as a project desired for the country at that time. We observed that disagreements over the conceptual and discursive frameworks established by Varnhagen – frameworks, which Capistrano de Abreu so gladly nominated by the expression "iron frames" – existed and will always be potentially prone to exist. However, the institution of Varnhagen as the authority of Brazilian national history and historiography remained guaranteed not only in situations when the general discursive lines of his work were ratified by his annotators, but also when criticisms were enunciated whilst still concerning the discursive matrix founded by the Viscount. Both criticism and ratification of the *General History of Brasil* discursive core worked to establish Francisco Adolfo de Varnhagen as an authority because both of them shared the same conceptual and discursive boundaries as if they were different sides of this huge historiographic wall.

When we roam the pages of the *General History of Brazil* through its margins, footnotes, and end of section notes, a new way for us to understand how Varnhagen became the major discursive authority regarding the Brazilian history and historiography. In doing so, we also can better understand the Brazilian history and history of historiography. The phenomenon of recognition essential to any relationship of authority is so present both as discourse-language and within the very own materiality of *General History of Brazil*. Therefore, the discourse on the " National History" of Brazil as proposed in Varnhagen's conceptual-discursive framework were perpetuated, appropriated, and updated to maintain the historical and historiographical foundation laid by him until at least mid-twentieth century. Helped by the *artífices* Capistrano de Abreu and Rodolfo Garcia, Francisco Adolfo de Varnhagen was able to ensure and enlarge the *auctoritas* he had founded over resilient iron frames.

Sources

ABREU, J. Capistrano. *Matching Capistrano de Abreu.Rio de Janeiro: National Book Institute, 1954-1956.*

(...) *Tests and studies: (criticism and history).1. Series.* Rio de Janeiro: Capistrano de Abreu Society, 1931.

(...) *Tests and studies: (criticism and history).*2. Series. Rio de Janeiro: Capistrano de Abreu Society, 1932.

(...) *Tests and studies: (criticism and history).*3. Series. Rio de Janeiro: Capistrano de Abreu Society, 1938.

BRANDÃO, Ambrose Fernandes. *Dialogues of the magnitudes of Brazil.*Rio de janeiro: [Tecnoprint] 1968.

CARDIM, Ferdinand. *Treaties of the land and people of Brazil.São Paulo: Companhia Editora Nacional, 1939.*

DIAS, Carlos Malheiro (Org.). *History of the Portuguese colonization of Brazil.Commemorative monumental edition of the first centennial of the Independence of Brazil.* Port: National Lithography / Publisher Society of History of Colonization Portuguese of Brazil, 1921-1924.

Gandavo, Magellanic Pero. *History of the Province* of *Santa Cruz; Treaty of the land of Brazil.*Sao Paulo: Obelisco, 1964.

GARCIA, Rodolfo. *Mr. inaugural Rodolfo Garcia.Rio de Janeiro: Brazilian Academy of Letters,* s/d. Available Text: http://www.academia.org.br/abl/cgi/cgilua.exe/sys/start.htm?infoid=8478&sid=350 . Accessed: 17/02/2011.

(...) *Writings loose.*Rio de Janeiro: Publications and Dissemination Division, 1973.

(...) *Systems bibliographic classification: Decimal classification and its advantages.*Rio de Janeiro: Brazilian Association of Librarians, 1969.

Mendoça, Heitor Furtado. *First visit of the Holy Officio parts of Brazil by the licensee Heitor Furtado Mendoça: Confessions of Bahia (1591-1592).*Rio de Janeiro: F. Briguiet, 1935.

(...) *First visit of the Holy Officio to* the *parties of Brazil by the licensee Heitor Furtado Mendoça: denunciations of Bahia (1591-1593).* São Paulo: Ed Paulo Prado, 1925..

(...) *First visit of the Holy Officio to* the *parties of Brazil by the licensee Heitor Furtado Mendoça: denunciations of Pernambuco (1593-1595)*. São Paulo: Ed Paulo Prado, 1929..

SALVADOR, Vicente's, Friar .*History of Brazil.*Sao Paulo: Improvements, [1931].

SOUSA, Pero Lopes. *Daily navigation Pero Lopes de Sousa: 1530-1532.*Rio de Janeiro: Typographia Leuzinger, 1927.

(...) *Daily Pero Lopes de Sousa navigation along the coast of Brazil to the Rio Uruguay (1530-1532).*Rio de Janeiro: DL Typographia dos Santos, 1867.

VARNHAGEN, Francisco Adolfo. *Examen de quelques points de l'histoire du Brésil géographique or analyze critique du rapport de M. d'Avezac sur la récente Histoire générale du Brésil.Paris: Imprimerie L. Martinet, 1858.*

(...) *General history of Brazil: before their separation and independence of Portugal.*3. ed. full. Sao Paulo: Improvements, [1927-1936].

(...) *General history of Brazil: before their separation and independence of Portugal.*4.ed. full. Sao Paulo: Improvements, 1948-1953.

References

ABREU, Martha, SOIHET, Rachel and GONTIJO, Rebecca (Eds.). *Political culture and readings of the past: history and teaching history. Rio de Janeiro: Brazilian Civilization, 2007.*

. LETTERS OF BRAZILIAN ACADEMY *Rodolfo Garcia - Biography.*Rio de Janeiro: Brazilian Academy of Letters, s / d..Available Text: http://www.academia.org.br/abl/cgi/cgilua.exe/sys/start.htm?infoid=212&sid=350. Accessed: 17/02/2011.

ANDERSON, Benedict. *Imagined Communities: reflexiones sobre el origen y la diffusion del nationalism.*Mexico City: Fonde of Economic Culture, 1993.

ALVES, Jorge Luis dos Santos. The memory of lusobrasileirismo in Brazilian history: the "History of Colonization Portuguese in Brazil. *Anais, Program and Abstracts of the XXVI Annual Meeting of the Brazilian Society of Historical Research.*Rio de Janeiro, 2006. http://sbph.org/reuniao/26/trabalhos/Jorge%20Luis%20Santos%20Alves.pdf
Accessed on 18/05/2010 at 15:10.

(...) *Malheiro Dias and the Portuguese-Brazilianism: a case study of cultural relations Brazil-Portugal.* Doctoral thesis. Advisor: Prof..Dra. Lúcia Maria Bastos Pereira das Neves.Rio de Janeiro: State University of Rio de Janeiro / Program Graduate in History, 2009.

ARAUJO, Ricardo Benzaquen of. Nightwatch: narrative, critical and truth in Capistrano de Abreu. *Historical Studies.Rio de Janeiro, n.1, p.28-54, 1988.*

Arendt, Hannah. *Between the past and the future.Sao Paulo: Perspective, 2007.*

CARVALHO, José *Murilo. The* construction of the order: the imperial political elite; Shadow theater: imperial policy.Rio de Janeiro: Brazilian Civilization, 2006.

CERTEAU, Michel. *The writing of history.Rio De Janeiro* to: University Forensic, 2006.

CEZAR, Themistocles. The geography served, first of all, to unify the Empire: Writing history and geographical knowledge in the nineteenth century Brazil. *Agora.Santa Cruz do Sul,* v.11, n.1, p.79-99, Jan./June, 2005.

(...) *L'écriture de l'histoire au Brésil au XIXe siècle: essai sur une rhétorique de la nacionalité: Le cas Varnhagen.Doctoral thesis.* Advisor: Prof. Dr. François Hartog. Paris: EHESS, 2002.

(...) When a manuscript becomes historical source: the true marks on account of Gabriel Soares de Souza (1587). *History magazine. Pellets,* v.6, p.37-58 ten. 2000.

(...) Varnhagen in movement: a brief anthology of an existence. *Topoi: Journal of History.* Rio de Janeiro: Graduate Program in Social History at UFRJ / 7Letras, v.8, n.15, p. 159-207, July-Dec., 2007.

DARBO-Peschanski, Catherine (Org.). *La citation dans l'Antiquité. Grenoble: Éditions Jérôme Millon, 2005.*

FOUCAULT, Didier & PAYEN, Pascal (Eds.). *Les Autorités. Dynamiques et mutations d'une figure de référence à l'Antiquité.Grenoble: Éditions Jérôme Millon, 2007.*

Foucault, Michel. *The archeology of knowledge.*Rio de Janeiro: University Forensic, 2009.

(...) *The order of discourse: inaugural lecture at the Collège de France, issued on December 2, 1970.* São Paulo: Loyola, 2008.

(...) *Words and things: an archeology of the human sciences.São Paulo: Martins Fontes, 1999.*

(...) *What is an author?* Lisbon: Vega Publisher 1997.

Gay, Peter. *The style in history: Gibbon, Ranke, Macaulay, Burckhardt. São Paulo: Companhia das Letras, 1990.*

Genette, Gerard. *Introduction to architext.*Lisbon: Vega Publisher 1987.

(...) *Seuils.Paris: Éditions du Seuil, 2007.*

GOMES, Angela de Castro. *The Republic, the history and IHGB.* Belo Horizonte: Argvmentvm 2009.

GONTIJO, Rebeca. Capistrano de Abreu, traveler. *Brazilian History magazine.São* Paulo, v.30, n.59, p.15-36, 2010.

(...) History and historiography in Abreu Capistrano cards. *History,* São Paulo, v.24, n.2, p.159-185, 2005.

(...) The "cross of intelligence": Capistrano de Abreu, memory and biography. *90: Graduate Program in History magazine,* Porto Alegre, v.14, n.26, p.41-76, ten, 2007..

GRAFTON, Anthony. *The footnote: a curious history*. Cambridge: Harvard University Press, 1997.

GUIMARAES, Lucia M. Paschoal. *Palatine school to silogeu: Brazilian Historical and Geographical Institute (1889-1938).Rio de Janeiro: Museum of the Republic, 2007.*

(...) Under the Immediate Proteca to His Imperial Majesty. The Institute Hist Orico and Geographic Brasileiro (1838-1889).*Journal of the Historical and Geographic Institute.R* io de Janeiro, a.156, v.1, n.388, p.459-613, jul./set., 1995.Text available http://www.ihgb. org.br/rihgb/rihgb1995numero0388.pdf . Accessed 27/09/2010.

(...) IV Congress of National History: trends and prospects in the history of colonial Brazil (Rio de Janeiro, 1949). *Brazilian History magazine.São* Paulo, v.24, n.48, p.145-170, 2004.Text available http://www.scielo.br/pdf/rbh/v24n48/a07v24n48.pdf. Accessed 29/09/2010.

(...) First Congress of National History: brief overview of the historiographical activity at the dawn of the twentieth century *Time Magazine.*. Rio de Janeiro, v.9, n.18, p.147-170, Jan. 2005.Text available http://www.historia.uff.br/tempo/artigos_livres/artg18-7. pdf. Accessed 29/09/2010.

(...) An unexpected partner: Historical and Geographical Brazilian Institute and the Royal Society of Northern Antiquaries. *Journal of the Historical and Geographic Institute.Rio de Janeiro, a.15* 5, v.1, n.384, p.479-498, jul./set. 1994.Text available http://www.ihgb. org.br/rihgb/rihgb1994numero0384.pdf . Accessed 27/09/2010.

GUIMARAES, Manoel Luiz Salgado (Org.). *Studies on the writing of history.Rio de Janeiro: 7Letras 2006.*

(...) Nation and civilization in the tropics: the Brazilian Historical and Geographical Institute and the project of a National History. *Historical Studies,* Rio de Janeiro, n.1, p.5-27, 1988.

GUMBRECHT, Hans Ulrich. *The functions of parliamentary rhetoric in the French Revolution: preliminary studies for a historical pragmatics of text.*Belo Horizonte: UFMG, 2003.

(...) *Modernization of the senses.São Paulo: Ed 34, 1998.*.

Hartog, François. *The Art of Historical Narrative* In: Boutier, Jean &

JULIA, Dominique (Eds.).*After recomposed: fields and plots of history.Rio de Ja* Neiro: Ed.UFRJ / Ed.FGV 1998, p.193-202.

(...) Évidence de lʹhistoire. Ce que les voient historiens.Paris: Gallimard / Éditions EHESS of 2005.

(...) *The nineteenth century and the history: the case of Fustel Coulanges. Rio de Janeiro: Ed.UFRJ 2003.*

(...) The disoriented Time, Time and History: "How to write the history of France?". *90: Graduate Program in History magazine.Porto Alegre*, n.7, p.7-28, July. 1997.

(...) *The old, the past and the present.*Brasilia: UNB Ed., 2003.

(...) *Historicity schemes: presenteeism and time experiences.Belo Horizonte: Authentic, 2013.*

HERCULANO, Aexandre. *Solemnia money: letters to Mr. AL Magessi Tavares on the current issue between the truth and a part of the clergy. Lisbon: National Press, 1850.*

HRUBY Hugo. The Historical and Geographical Brazilian Institute on the threshold of the Republic (1889-1912): decisive moments. *Proceedings of the IX Meeting of State History ANPUH / RS.* Porto Alegre: ANPUH / RS, 2008.Text available at: http://www.eeh2008. anpuh-rs.org.br/resources/content/anais/1212158581_ARQUIVO_HugoHruby.pdf. Accessed 06/12/2010.

(...) The temple of the holy scriptures: the Historical and Geographical Brazilian Institute and the writing of the history of Brazil (1889-1912). *History of Historiography,* Ouro Preto, n.2, p.50-66, sea. 2009.Text available at: http://www.ichs.ufop.br/rhh/index. php/revista/article/viewFile/7/7. Accessed 06/12/2010.

Kojève, Alexandre. *La notion d'autorité.Paris: Éditions* Gallimard, 2004.

Koselleck, Reinhart. *Future Past contribution to the semantics of historical times.Rio de Janeiro: Counterpoint / Ed.PUCRJ 2006.*

_____. *Historia / history.Madrid: Editorial Trotta, 2004.*

LE GOFF, Jacques. *History and memory.Campinas: Ed.UNICAMP, 2003.*

LIMA, Luiz Costa. *History. Fiction. Literature.* São Paulo: Company of letters, 2006.

MATTOS, Ilmar Rohloff. Capistrano chapters .In: *Modern Discove-*

ries of Brazil. Text available at: http://www.historiaecultura.pro.br/modernosdescobrimentos/desc/capistrano/frame.htm . Accessed 19/09/2010.

(...) *The Saquarema time.Sao Paulo: Hucitec; [Brasilia, DF]: INL, 1987.*

MATTOS, Selma Rinaldi. *The lessons in Brazil: history as a school subject in Joaquim Manuel de Macedo.Rio de Janeiro: Access 2000.*

MOLLO, Helena Miranda. *General History of Brazil: between space and time* In: COSTA, Wilma Peres & OLIVEIRA, Cecilia Helena Salles (Eds.).*Of an empire to another, formation of Brazil, eighteenth and nineteenth centuries.* Sao Paulo: Hucitec: FAPESP, 2007 p.99-118.

Momigliano, Arnaldo. *The classical roots of modern historiography.*Bauru: EDUSC 2004.

OLIVEIRA, Maria da Glória. The annotation and writing: about the story in the capítul John Capistrano de Abreu.*History of Historiography,* n.2, p.86-99, sea. 2009.Text available at: http://www.ichs.ufop.br/rhh/index.php/revista/article/viewFile/9/9. Accessed 01/10/2010.

(...) *Critical method and writing the story in John Capistrano de Abreu (1853-1927).Masters dissertation. Advisor: Prof. Dr. Themistocles Cezar. Porto Alegre: UFRGS, IFCH - Department of History, Graduate Program in History, 2006.*

PEIRCE, Charles Sanders. *Semiotics.Sao Paulo: Perspective, 2003.*

PEREIRA, Daniel Mosque. *Capistrano discoveries: the history of Brazil "the great features and large - mesh".*Doctoral thesis. The rientador: Prof.Dr. Ilmar Rohloff de Mattos.Rio de Janeiro: PUC, Department of History, 2002.

PROST, Antoine. *Twelve lessons on history.Belo Horizonte: Authentic Publishing, 2008.*

Revault D'Allonnes, Myriam. *El poder de los comienzos. Ensayo sobre la autoridad.Buenos Aires: Amorrortu 2008.*

Ricoeur, Paul. *Memory, history, oblivion.Campinas: Editora da Unicamp, 2007.*

(...) *Teoría de la interpretación. Speech y surplus of meaning.Mexico City: Siglo XXI Editores, 2006.*

RODRIGUES, Jose Honorio. *Historical research in Brazil.*São Paulo:

Companhia Editora Nacional 1969.

(...) *History of the history of Brazil.* São Paulo: Companhia Editora Nacional, 1978-1988.

(...) *History and historiography.Petropolis: Voices, 1970.*

(...) *Theory of the history of Brazil: methodological introduction.São Paulo: Ed National., 1969.*

(...) Varnhagen: the first master of Brazilian historiography (1816-1878). *America History magazine.Mexico, n.88, jul./dez., 1979 p.93-122.*

Rüsen, Jörn. *Living history. Theory of history: forms and functions of historical knowledge.*Brasília: Editora UNB, 2007.

(...) *historical reason. History of theory: the fundamentals of historical science.Brasília: Editora UNB, 2001.*

(...) *Reconstruction of the past.History of theory: the principles of historical research.Brasília: Editora UNB, 200 7.*

Sahlins, Marshall. *History Islands.*Rio de Janeiro: Jorge Zahar Editor, 2003.

Schwarcz, Lilia Moritz. *The spectacle of the races: scientists, institutions and race in Brazil: 1870-1930.*São Paulo: Companhia das Letras, 1993.

SCHWARZ, Roberto. *To the victor the potatoes: literary form and social process in the Brazilian novel beginnings.Sao Paulo: Two Cities, 1988.*

Sevcenko, Nicholas. *Literature mission: social tensions and cultural creation in the First Republic.São Paulo: Companhia das Letras, 2003.*

SILVA, Itala Byanca M. da. Annotate and prefacing the work of the "master": reflections of Jose Honorio Rodrigues on Capistrano de Abreu. *History of Historiography,* n.3, p.83-105, Sept.. 2009.Text available at: http://www.ichs.ufop.br/rhh/index.php/revista/article/viewFile/55/35. Accessed 04/01/2011.

(...) The Abreu Capistrano disciples: Paulo Prado and the "Sea Way." *Anais, Program and Abstracts of the XXVI Annual Meeting of the Brazilian Society of Historical Research.Rio de Janeiro: 2006.* Text available at: http://sbph.org/reuniao/26/trabalhos/Jorge%20Luis%20Santos%20Alves.pdf .Accessed 18/05/2010.

SOUZA, Antonio Cândido de Mello and. *Formation of Brazilian literature: decisive moments 1750-1880.* Rio de Janeiro: FAPESP /

Gold over blue, 2007.

Sussekind Plant. *Brazil is not far from here: the narrator, the journey.São Paulo: Companhia das Letras, 1990.*

Sussekind, Plant & DIAS, Tania (Eds.). *The literary historiography and writing techniques: From manuscript to* **hypertext.Rio de Janeiro: Publishing House of Rui Barbosa: Vieira and Lent, 2004.**

TURIN, Rodrigo. *Narrating the past, designing the future: Romero and nineteenth-century historiography experience.Masters dissertation. Advisor: Prof. Dr. Themistocles Cezar. Porto Alegre: UFRGS, IFCH - Department of History, Graduate Program in History, 2005.*

Uricoechea, Fernando. *The imperial minotaur: the bureaucratization of the Brazilian equity state in the nineteenth century.* Rio de Janeiro: Difel 1978.

VENTURA, Roberto. *Tropical style: cultural history and literary polemics in Brazil, 1870-1914.São Paulo: Companhia das Letras, 199* 1.

Veyne, Paul. *How to write the story; Foucault revolutionizes history.B* rasília: Publisher UNB, 2008.

WALDER, Dennis (Ed.). *Literature in the Modern World: Critical Essays and Documents.*New York, Oxford University Press / The Open University, 1990.

Wehling Arno. *The invention of history: studies of historicism.Niteroi UFF Ed., 1994.*

(...) *State, history, memory: Varnhagen and the construction of national identity.*Rio de Janeiro: New Frontier 1999.

WHITE, Hayden. *Metahistory: the historical imagination in nineteenth-century Europe.* Baltimore / London: The Johns Hopkins University Press, 1975.

(...) *Speech Tropics: Essays on the critique of culture.* São Paulo: EDUSP, 1974.

www.ingramcontent.com/pod-product-compliance
Lightning Source LLC
LaVergne TN
LVHW041222080426
835508LV00011B/1043